AF799625

# The Demand for Life Insurance

Wookjae Heo

# The Demand for Life Insurance

## Dynamic Ecological Systemic Theory Using Machine Learning Techniques

palgrave
macmillan

Wookjae Heo
South Dakota State University
Brookings, SD, USA

ISBN 978-3-030-36902-6 ISBN 978-3-030-36903-3 (eBook)
https://doi.org/10.1007/978-3-030-36903-3

© The Editor(s) (if applicable) and The Author(s), under exclusive license to Springer Nature Switzerland AG 2020
This work is subject to copyright. All rights are solely and exclusively licensed by the Publisher, whether the whole or part of the material is concerned, specifically the rights of translation, reprinting, reuse of illustrations, recitation, broadcasting, reproduction on microfilms or in any other physical way, and transmission or information storage and retrieval, electronic adaptation, computer software, or by similar or dissimilar methodology now known or hereafter developed.
The use of general descriptive names, registered names, trademarks, service marks, etc. in this publication does not imply, even in the absence of a specific statement, that such names are exempt from the relevant protective laws and regulations and therefore free for general use.
The publisher, the authors and the editors are safe to assume that the advice and information in this book are believed to be true and accurate at the date of publication. Neither the publisher nor the authors or the editors give a warranty, expressed or implied, with respect to the material contained herein or for any errors or omissions that may have been made. The publisher remains neutral with regard to jurisdictional claims in published maps and institutional affiliations.

Cover illustration: © John Rawsterne/patternhead.com

This Palgrave Pivot imprint is published by the registered company Springer Nature Switzerland AG
The registered company address is: Gewerbestrasse 11, 6330 Cham, Switzerland

# Preface

It was difficult to combine multiple disciplines—consumer economics, financial planning, and computer sciences—into a book. The conceptual linkages among these fields were not easily made. However, these fields have different theories with a high number of similarities: ecological systemic theory, dynamic concepts from chaos theory, and neural networks algorithms. All of these theories and concepts indicate, or imply, that various factors connected to the consumers are inter- and intra-related. Based on the similarities among these theories, it was possible to combine the different disciplines into one conceptual approach in this book.

This book is important for two reasons. First, it presents a comprehensive understanding about the demand for life insurance. The book starts by providing a general explanation about risk and risk management, which are the foundational concepts for life insurance. By understanding the comprehensive concepts of risk and risk management, readers can understand why life insurance should be understood while considering the various influential factors related to consumers.

Second, there is a theoretical linkage among consumer economics, financial planning, and computer science. Previously, few efforts were made to link social/behavioral science and computer science to establish a new theoretical linkage.

In this book, this theoretical linkage is suggested as a new conceptual framework for understanding the demand for life insurance. With this research trial, the researchers might find a pathway to combine social/behavioral sciences with the computer sciences.

The analytical parts should be read as practical examples for the use of this new conceptual framework, which is the empirical extension of a theoretical linkage between social/behavioral sciences and computer sciences. However, the analytics of consumer sciences technology can be improved because many computer scientists are rapidly developing new analytical technologies. Therefore, gaining an understanding of this part of the analytical procedure is the initial example to follow for learning how best to use the new conceptual framework (i.e., theoretical linkage between social/behavioral sciences and computer sciences) empirically.

I would like to thank Dr. John E. Grable because he has been a great supporter for me to develop the theoretical linkage between social/behavioral sciences and computer sciences. Also, I thank Dr. Lance Palmer and Dr. Swarn Chatterjee for giving advices on these contents. My thanks go out to my friends, family, and colleagues: Mr. Sooho Heo, Ms. Jassuk Han, Mr. Jungduk Choi, Ms. Junglan Lee, Dr. JunHyuck Choi, Dr. Kristi Warren Scott, Dr. Jae Min Lee, Dr. Narang Park, Dr. Anthony L. Mescher, and Dr. Joseph C. Miller. Finally, a special thank you goes out to Ms. Jeong Hyun Choi.

Brookings, SD, USA Wookjae Heo

# Contents

# List of Figures

# List of Tables

CHAPTER 1

# Introduction: A Need of New Framework in Financial Planning with the Case of Life Insurance Demand

**Abstract** This chapter is a general introduction to the issue of understanding life insurance and demand for it in the market. Unlike the actuarial science and lifespan-related economic approaches, this book was based on a different analytical framework to understand the demand for life insurance. By using a machine learning technique and the complexities among influential determinant factors, it may be possible to predict the demand for life insurance more accurately. To justify the usage of machine learning in financial planning, a new theoretical framework is briefly introduced in this chapter.

**Keywords** Life insurance · Demand for life insurance · Complexity in insurance market · Dynamic nonlinear systemic approach

## 1.1 Introduction and Statement of the Problem

The life insurance market is large, dynamic, and somewhat fragmented. Consider the following facts from the Insurance Information Institute (2015) and LIMRA (2014):

- Life insurance has been sold in the United States for over 200 years;
- Consumers paid nearly $164 billion in life insurance premiums in 2013;

© The Author(s) 2020

W. Heo, *The Demand for Life Insurance*,
https://doi.org/10.1007/978-3-030-36903-3_1

- The five largest insurers (i.e., MetLife, Prudential, New York Life, TIAA-CREF, and Northwestern Mutual) each have revenues that exceed $24,000 million;
- Only 49% of consumers age 25–64 own individual life insurance;
- Fifty percent of the adult US population say they need life insurance;
- Nearly 90% of consumers believe life insurance is too expensive to purchase;
- Approximately 10% of the US population plans to purchase a life insurance policy within the next year; and
- Forty percent of consumers report that a life event (e.g., death of family member or close friend, getting married or divorced, etc.) prompted them to purchase life insurance.

These insurance details highlight the diverse nature of the life insurance marketplace. On the one hand, the insurance industry has a long history in the United States and is today a multi-billion dollar business. On the other hand, life insurance, as an important financial planning product, has limited market penetration. This helps explain why much of the existing life insurance research has been devoted to understanding the pricing mechanisms of life insurance and sales delivery and purchasing trends among consumers. The life insurance industry has been preoccupied with identifying pricing strategies that will attract new consumers to the insurance marketplace. A quick glance at the insurance industry's leading Web sites and trade publications shows that industry groups spend a great deal of time, effort, and resources attempting to document life insurance ownership patterns and possibilities.

As will be discussed in this chapter, nearly all previous studies that have focused on the demand for life insurance have been conceptualized from a supply-side perspective. This study attempts to reframe the discussion of life insurance demand by conceptualizing the demand for life insurance as being shaped by many interrelated factors. Further, this study is premised on the notion that these factors can best be modeled using advanced statistical techniques that rely on artificial neural network techniques. This chapter provides a broad overview of the models most often used to predict and explain demand for life insurance among consumers, the factors most often hypothesized to be useful in predicting demand, and the conceptualization of this research. Later chapters provide a review of the relevant literature, a discussion of the research methodology, results from the statistical analyses, and an applied discussion.

It is important to start any discussion about life insurance demand by clarifying the role of life insurance within a consumer's financial plan. Essentially, life insurance serves as a precaution for an unexpected event like the premature death of a family's breadwinner, providing protection for the loss of a member of a household is the main reason people should, and most often do, purchase life insurance (Rejda, 2008; Thoyts, 2010). Losing a household's breadwinner critically increases the financial vulnerability of a household, since the major source of income disappears with the death of the breadwinner. Even if the person who dies is not the household's breadwinner, the loss of a related household member generates various economic burdens on the other members in the household. For instance, the premature death of a household member could leave unpaid medical bills and possible debt to be paid by others in the household (Rejda, 2008). These examples illustrate how life insurance works as a tool for managing the risk of premature death in a household.

When attempting to understand how life insurance works as a financial buffer against financial disaster, it is important to predict who will be more likely to purchase life insurance and the factors that lead people to purchase life insurance. Specifically, financial planners provide consulting advice on the purchase of appropriate life insurance policies based, in part, on their clients' socioeconomic situation. Financial planners need valid, reliable tools to predict which people would like to purchase life insurance and the kinds of factors that are associated with purchasing behavior. In addition, policy makers have a need to understand the reason people purchase insurance and the manner in which people decide to purchase. This interest is premised on the notion that political issues, such as Social Security funding, are strongly related to the purchase of life insurance (Black & Skipper, 2000). Policy makers need to enforce market controls to help the market work efficiently and effectively. Furthermore, educators and researchers need information about consumers and purchase decision factors because predicting the demand for life insurance is one possible way to increase consumers' financial well-being (Lynch, 2010).

There have been two major approaches used by researchers to understand the demand for life insurance: (a) actuarial science and (b) lifespan-related economic perspectives (e.g., human capital theory and the life cycle hypothesis). Actuarial science and lifespan-related economics are well developed and easily adapted for the use in understanding and explaining the life insurance market. For instance, these two major approaches explain well the price of life insurance and the quantity of selling in the real market. However, these approaches have serious limitations. These approaches tend to focus on finding and explaining the macro-level equilibrium in the real market rather than identifying and predicting influential factors in the decision-making process at the household level. In other words, actuarial science and lifespan-related economics are premised on different analytical purposes to estimate the equilibrium between demand and supply. These analytical approaches are not as efficient when predicting influential demand factors (i.e., which people tend to purchase life insurance and the factors associated with life insurance purchase decisions).

Specifically, actuarial life insurance theories, like financial models, mortality models, net single premium functions, and multiple discretion models, use limited specific factors to estimate the demand for life insurance. Typical inputs include factors such as present value, longevity, death rates, and cancellation ratios. Since actuarial life insurance theories were developed from an industrial perspective (i.e., supply-side), actuarial models focus on appropriate premium rates for life insurance. It is worth exploring this approach. The actuarial approach tends to rely on one of the following functions: (a) present value of time capital from financial models, (b) survivor function, and (c) net single premium function. The formula for each method is shown below:

$$\mathrm{AC} = c_1 v^{t1} + c_2 v^{t2} + \cdots + c_k v^{tk} \tag{1.1}$$

$$s(\chi) = 1 - F_X(\chi) = \Pr[X > \chi] \tag{1.2}$$

$$E[Z] = \int_0^{\infty} b_t v_t^t p_\chi \mu_\chi(t)\mathrm{d}t \tag{1.3}$$

For function (1.1), $c$ denotes the present value, $v$ means the discount factor associated with time ($t$), and t is the time period. The present value for time capital (AC) is the same as the sum of the time series' values. For function (1.2), $X$ denotes a distribution of lifetimes among the population, where $\chi$ means people who survive at the age of $\chi$. The survivor function indicates the probability a person survives until the age of $\chi$. For function (1.3), $v$ is the discount factor associated with time ($t$), $b$ is the insurance benefit, $p_\chi$ is the surviving probability until the age of

$\chi$, and $\mu_{\chi}$ is the mortality probability at the age of $\chi$. Expected net single premium ($E[Z]$) is the integration of insurance benefits, surviving and mortality probabilities, and the discount factor. As shown in these three functions, actuarial science is focused on projecting longevity and associated costs. These are appropriate tools to estimate the price of life insurance. However, from the consumer's perspective, the actuarial science method is not an efficient tool when answering the following two questions: (a) Which people tend to purchase life insurance and (b) what factors are associated with the decision to purchase life insurance?

For the case of the lifespan-related economic perspective (e.g., life cycle model and human capital theory), economic factors like price and quantity of life insurance in the market are considered in the demand function and utility function, respectively. Since the lifespan-related economic perspective focuses on the utilities created in a market, optimal price and quantity are the main outcomes associated with economic life insurance research. The following functions represent the life cycle hypothesis and human capital model equation:

$$C = aW + bY \tag{1.4}$$

$$P = MP + G = W + C = \pi \tag{1.5}$$

For the life cycle hypothesis function (1.4), consumption (C) is the same as the sum of marginal propensity to consume (a) for wealth (W) and the marginal propensity to consume (b) for income (Y). For the human capital model function (1.5), P denotes total labor productivity, MP denotes marginal productivity, G denotes excess of future receipts, W denotes wage, C denotes sum of opportunity costs for training or education, and $\pi$ denotes the total wage. Equation (1.5) shows that if there is education or training for a worker ($P = MP + G$), the effect of education or training will generate a return as more productivity and total wage ($W + C = \pi$). Similar to the actuarial science approach, classical economic approaches can be used to understand the macro-level equilibrium in a market. However, from the perspective of consumer behavior, economic approaches are less than optimal in showing which people tend to purchase life insurance and the factors that are associated with the purchase of life insurance.

Although these two perspectives focus on finding a market-oriented equilibrium, many researchers have attempted to investigate the determinants of life insurance demand based upon these two perspectives (e.g., Anderson & Nevin, 1975; Babbel, 1985; Berekson, 1972; Browne & Kim, 1993; Burnett & Palmer, 1984; Chen, Wong, & Lee, 2001; Duker, 1969; Ferber & Lee, 1980; Fitzgerald, 1987; Gandolfi & Miners, 1996; Gutter & Hatcher, 2008; Hammond, Houston, & Melander, 1967; Hau, 2000; Lewis, 1989; Liebenberg, Carson, & Dumm, 2012; Mantis & Farmer, 1968; Showers & Shotick, 1994; Williams, 1986; Zietz, 2003). Using these empirical and practical approaches, researchers have noted diverse possible determinant factors, such as age, gender, family structure, and wealth on the demand for life insurance. Results from the literature illustrate that there are a number of diverse determinants associated with the demand for life insurance.

However, there is still a limitation associated with the common approaches used in most widely used empirical models; namely, there has been no consistent, uniform specific framework for selecting predictor variables. With the lack of a consistent framework, models of the determinant factors change with each empirical study. Zietz (2003) noted that this can create some confusing and controversial results. Table 1.1 shows how previous findings from the literature tend to be contradictory and at times opposite of traditional assumptions.

As shown in Table 1.1, many variables exhibit contradictory and controversial associations with the demand for life insurance. Some variables (e.g., education, income, and inflation/interest rates) show bipolar directional associations (i.e., positive and negative association) with life insurance demand. A few other variables, including wife working status and family size/family structure, show one of three possible results: positive association, negative association, and non-significant association. Other variables, such as life expectancy, marital status, religion, net worth, and employment, rarely show consistent results.

Besides the associations shown in Table 1.1, the relationships among other variables and the demand for life insurance often lead to conflicting findings. For instance, Showers and Shotick (1994) found age had a positive association with the demand for life insurance. However, Chen et al. (2001) found age was negatively related to the demand for life insurance. It is possible to assume, because of many factor changes, covariance and interaction terms among selected determinant factors become unstable depending on the research model. Therefore, previous research findings on the determinant factors of life insurance should be expected to show inconsistent results. These inconsistencies restrict more accurate predictions of the demand for life insurance.

**Table 1.1** Controversial research findings related to life insurance demand

| *Variable* | *Positively significant association* | *Negatively significant association* | *Non-significant association* |
|---|---|---|---|
| Education | Hammond et al. (1967)<br>Ferber and Lee (1980)<br>Burnett and Palmer (1984)<br>Truett and Truett (1990)<br>Brown and Kim (1993)<br>Gandolfi and Miners (1996) | Duker (1996)<br>Anderson and Nevin (1975) | |
| Family size/ Family structure | Ferber and Lee (1980)<br>Burnett and Palmer (1984)<br>Lewis (1989)<br>Browne and Kim (1993)<br>Showers and Shotick (1994) | Hammond et al. (1967)<br>Mantis and Farmer (1968) | Duker (1969)<br>Anderson and Nevin (1975) |
| Life expectancy | Williams (1986) | | Browne and Kim (1993) |
| Marital status (1 = Married) | Lewis (1989) | Hammond et al. (1967)<br>Mantis and Falmer (1968) | Burnett and Palmer (1984) |
| Religion | | Burnett and Palmer (1984) | Browne and Kim (1993) |
| Wife working status | Ferber and Lee (1980)<br>Showers and Shotick (1994) | Duker (1969)<br>Gandolfi and Miners (1996) | Burnett and Palmer (1984) |
| Income | Hammond et al. (1967)<br>Mantis and Farmer (1968)<br>Duker (1969)<br>Ferber and Lee (1980)<br>Burnett and Palmer (1984)<br>Truett and Truett (1990)<br>Browne and Kim (1993)<br>Showers and Shotick (1994)<br>Gandolfi and Miners (1996) | Anderson and Nevin (1975): partially, on mid-income range | |
| Net worth | Hammond et al. (1967)<br>Duker (1969)<br>Anderson and Nevin (1975)<br>Ferber and Lee (1980)<br>Lewis (1989)<br>Eisenhauer and Hayek (1999)<br>Hau (2000)<br>Heo et al. (2013) | | Fitzgerald (1987) |

(continued)

**Table 1.1** (continued)

| *Variable* | *Positively significant association* | *Negatively significant association* | *Non-significant association* |
|---|---|---|---|
| Employment | Hammond et al. (1967)<br>Mantis and Farmer (1968)<br>Duker (1969)<br>Ferber and Lee (1980)<br>Fitzgerald (1987) | | Anderson and Nevin (1975) |
| Inflation/ Interest rate | Mantis and Farmer (1968) | Browne and Kim (1993) | |

*Note* Table adapted from "An examination of the demand for life insurance," by E. N. Zietz, 2003, *Risk management and insurance review*, 6, pp. 159–191. Copyright 2003 by Wiley

In order to better predict the demand for life insurance, it is necessary to adopt a more robust, consistent, and conceptual methodological framework that is able to combine a solid theoretical background as well as empirically determined features. This means moving beyond traditional supply-side frameworks to ones that take into account the interrelated nature of demand variables. Based on an understanding of the two traditional classical perspectives and empirical applications, this study will explore a new framework to explain which people tend to purchase life insurance and why people purchase life insurance. The framework is based on a dynamic nonlinear systemic approach, which will be discussed later in this chapter. Within this dynamic, nonlinear, and systemic approach, many determinants for life insurance demand are assumed to be interdependently correlated. The outcomes from this study will provide a better understanding of the factors associated with life insurance demand from a consumer's perspective. This study will ultimately provide a higher prediction level for the demand for life insurance.

## 1.2 Purpose and Justification of Study

Compared to the actuarial science and lifespan-related economics approaches, this study was based on a different analytical framework to understand the demand for cash value life insurance. By using the complexities among influential determinant factors, it may be possible to predict the demand for life insurance more accurately. As explained in the problem statement, the actuarial science and economic perspectives have often produced conflicting results. As a result, this study was designed using a more suitable theoretical framework to predict the demand for life insurance.

### *1.2.1 Complexity Among the Determinants of the Demand for Life Insurance*

Among published empirical research findings (e.g., Anderson & Nevin, 1975; Browne & Kim, 1993; Burnett & Palmer, 1984; Duker, 1969; Ferber & Lee, 1980; Fischer, 1973; Gandolfi & Miners, 1996; Hammond et al., 1967; Hau, 2000; Heo, Grable, & Chatterjee, 2013; Lewis, 1989; Mantis & Famer, 1968; Showers & Shotick, 1994), it is common to find inconsistent results in prediction models for the demand for life insurance. Some socio-demographic factors (e.g., education, family structure, and spouse working status) show conflicting results as opposite influential effects on the demand for life insurance. In terms of education, many researchers have found a positive association between years of education and life insurance demand (Browne & Kim, 1993; Burnett & Palmer, 1984; Ferber & Lee, 1980; Gandolfi & Miners, 1996; Hammond et al., 1967). However, there have been a few reports showing a negative association between education and life insurance demand (e.g., Anderson & Nevin, 1975; Duker, 1969). Similar conflicts exist in relation to family structure. Family size and the number of children are generally thought to be positively related to life insurance demand. Some researchers have documented a positive association (e.g., Browne & Kim, 1993; Burnett & Palmer, 1984; Ferber & Lee, 1980). However, a few other researchers have noted that family size and the number of children show a negative relation with life insurance demand (e.g., Hammond et al., 1967; Mantis & Famer, 1968). Similarly, the working status of a spouse can be positively related to life insurance demand (Ferber & Lee 1980; Showers & Shotick, 1994), but it can be negatively associated with the life insurance demand as well (Burnett & Palmer, 1984; Duker, 1969; Gandolfi & Miners, 1996).

In addition to the inconsistent associations among socio-demographic variables, family financial variables (e.g., wealth and social security) also have debatable associations with the demand for life insurance. As originally conceptualized, life insurance demand should be negatively associated with wealth; that is, life insurance should work as a form of self-insurance (Fischer, 1973; Lewis, 1989). However, many empirical studies (e.g., Duker, 1969; Ferber & Lee, 1980; Hammond et al., 1967; Hau, 2000; Heo et al., 2013) have shown that wealth is positively associated with life insurance demand. The association between social security and life insurance demand is also controversial. Browne and Kim (1993) found that the association is positive, but Lewis (1989) argued that the association is negative. As a result, it is reasonable to hypothesize that many family financial variables can be ambiguous factors related to estimating life insurance demand.

Furthermore, psychological factors can be conflicting and ambiguous. Although the existence of risk is the main reason for purchasing insurance, it is not quite correct to state that the human response against risk leads to purchasing insurance (Thoyts, 2010). The human response to risk is associated with various factors, such as a person's perception of risk, the perception of reward, and the individual propensity to take risks. Therefore, there is no clear association between human response to risk and insurance purchases (Chesney & Louberge, 1986; Eisenhauer & Halek, 1999). Some researchers have reported that risk-averse households tend to be more likely to buy insurance (e.g., Berkovitch & Venezia 1992; Cleeton & Zellner, 1993); other researchers note that risk-tolerant people are more likely to purchase insurance (e.g., Xiao, 1996). The key point from these research findings is the management of risk which is a main factor for purchasing life insurance. Around the existence of risk, diverse factors, such as psychological factors and economic status, correlate with each other and often lead to the purchase of insurance.

To sum up, there are equivocal conflicting notions between life insurance demand and the influential determinant factors of demand (e.g., socio-demographic factors, family financial factors, and psychological factors). The problem is to understand how various characteristics and variables correlate with each other and how the correlations among diverse factors are related to the life insurance purchase decision. Any useful framework used to identify the determinant factors for life insurance demand should include a holistic understanding of the complexities consumers face in actuality.

Inconsistent findings reported in previous empirical studies may be caused by the complexities of the actual world. Each empirical research study is based on different assumptions regarding predicting factors. Few empirical studies have considered two important assumptions associated with estimating life insurance demand: (a) endogeneity, which can occur by dismissing significant factors on a model, and (b) overlooking inter-correlations among possible factors associated with the demand for life insurance. It is reasonable to assume that life insurance factors can provide diverse types of associations within models of the demand for life insurance. Associations could vary directly, indirectly, linearly, quadratically, and complicatedly. For instance, in the case of an indirect association, any insignificant factor in a statistical model could be a hidden factor, as a mediator, or a moderator. Traditional models would likely miss this possibility. Gutter and Hatcher (2008), for example, reviewed racial differences on the ownership of life insurance. Their findings did not show significantly different proportions for ownership of life insurance based on race (i.e., African-Americans and Caucasians). However, considering education levels as a proxy for human capital, African-American households insured a lower proportion of their human capital than Caucasian households. Regarding human capital, as indicated by education level, the findings changed from a non-significant relationship to a significant association.

In addition, Lu and Yanagihara (2013) explained that three macroeconomic factors are associated with each other: (a) growth rate, (b) educational investment, and (c) life insurance. According to their findings, purchasing life insurance positively promotes educational investment. Purchasing life insurance could show a positive association with the growth rate of a country. It is well known, for insurance, that educational investment (i.e., so-called human capital accumulation) is strongly associated with economic growth (Becker, 1962; Schultz, 1961). Linked with the strong relationship between education investment and growth rates, life insurance could be expected to work as a mediating factor to increase both investments and growth rates. This implies that factors related to life insurance demand likely do not have a simple direct, linear association, but instead have a complicated dynamic association.

### 1.2.2 *Adoption of a Dynamic Nonlinear Systemic Approach*

Over the past century, there has been an academic trend to understand the complexities of the actual world (Brenner, 1999). Originally, the trend started in the natural sciences, but this approach has been adopted into other social, economic, and finance fields (Brenner, 1999; Casti, 1992; Dechert, 1996; Goodwin, 1990; Kovalerchuk & Vityaev, 2000; Pines, 1988). A broad description of this academic trend can be explained with three concepts: (a) A social or economic structure has holistic deterministic rules that dominate the patterns inside structure; (b) the patterns inside the structure are structure-resembled, but randomly occurring alterations; and (c) these alterations occur by interdependent interactions from various influential factors. For instance, in the natural sciences, there is a deterministic rule that water flows from high to low. Because of the holistic rule, streams and rivers have similar shapes, but totally different alterations. No two streams or rivers have the same shape in reality. This is caused by many diverse environmental factors (e.g., diversity of rocks, altitudes, variety of plants, etc.) that interdependently interact.

Since various fields of study have adopted these new methods, respectively, the names of the approaches vary—evolutionary economics (Kwaśnicki, 1999), nonlinear science (Brock, 1996), and theory of chaotic dynamics (Dechert, 1996; Pines, 1988). Consequently, the associated methodologies are called by different names—data mining, machine learning, and nonlinear science. Because of various names and meanings, this study unifies these names into the following term: the dynamic nonlinear systemic approach. A detailed explanation for this nomenclature will be explained later. Regardless of the various names, all adoptions from diverse fields have uniform purposes and goals. The purposes and goals are to make possible predictions and estimations of holistic patterns in reality. As such, the dynamic nonlinear systemic approach will be used as the conceptual and methodological approach for this study.

## 1.3 Research Questions and Hypotheses

Based on the statement of problem and the purpose of study, this study focuses on the improvement of estimating the demand for life insurance. As previously explained, earlier approaches (e.g., actuarial science and lifespan-associated economics) provide a good approach for estimating life insurance demand when viewed from a market-oriented perspective, but these approaches are less efficient when estimating life insurance demand from a consumer behavioral perspective. Therefore, this study employs a new methodology—dynamic nonlinear systemic framework—for estimating life insurance demand from a consumer behavioral perspective.

The primary question of interest in this study is as follows: Does the usage of a dynamic nonlinear systemic (e.g., an artificial neural network) framework improve the prediction rate for the demand for life insurance compared to other econometric models (e.g., regression and logistic)? A secondary question is as follows: Does the categorizing of people into sub-samples (i.e., clustering) improve the discovery of influential variables on the demand for life insurance? A third question is as follows: What factors, from a consumer perspective, are most important when determining life insurance demand?

By answering the questions, this study helps expand the understanding of what variables influence cash value life insurance demand. Specifically, by utilizing nonlinear estimation with sub-sampling (i.e., combination of clustering analysis and ANN), the study identified more influential items related to dropping and purchasing life insurance. The result will give some implications to financial planners and researchers with the circumstance that could be results of using the dynamic non-linear systemic framework. For instance, financial planners need tools to predict which people will likely drop or purchase life insurance in the future. In addition, they need to know different factors associated with purchasing behavior. To this point, financial planners may use the findings from this study to better understand more about why people drop or purchase life insurance. As will be shown in Chapter 6, the high impact weight variables from the study can be used to gauge future behavior. As a result, the findings from this study support better prediction performance on the demand for life insurance, so the related people (financial planner, researchers in personal finance, and policy makers) can better understand which variables are the foundation for dropping and purchasing cash value life insurance.

## 1.4 Specific Research Objectives

There are two objectives associated with this study. First, as explained earlier, previous econometric models have often overlooked inter-correlations among possible factors associated with the demand for life insurance. These models use a linear assumption between the dependent variable and independent variables. In addition, these models assume that influential factors (i.e., independent variables) should be perfectly independent from each other (Halcousis, 2005). On the other hand, in actuality, consumer behavior is not simply based on linear associations. Rather, consumer behavior can show nonlinearity with interdependent correlations among influential factors on the demand for life insurance.

Thus, the first objective of this study is to test the nonlinear assumption (i.e., inter-correlated influential variables) related to life insurance demand. Second, artificial neural networks assume all possible influential factors are interrelated to each other, regardless of the strength of the relationship. The second objective of this study, based on the first objective, is to test a method, using artificial neural networks, to improve the prediction rate of the demand for life insurance. Finally, it is anticipated that factors of importance in predicting the demand for life insurance can be identified.

In this study, the general explanation will introduce the basic concepts of life insurance including term and cash value life insurance. However, at the empirical analytic part from Chapters 5 to 7, cash value life insurance will be analyzed. Since cash value life insurance (e.g., whole life insurance) deals with cash value by obtaining policy, but the term life insurance (i.e., pure insurance) does not provide a cash value, the demand for life insurance may differ between two types of life insurance. Therefore, it needs to focus on one specific type of life insurance among them. In this study, cash value life insurance was selected and analyzed as an example of utilizing the new conceptual framework (i.e., dynamic nonlinear systemic framework) in order to understand the demand for life insurance. In addition, group life insurance is an insurance that covers many people under one contract (Rejda, 2008). Because of this characteristic, group life insurance was not evaluated in the study.

## References


Anderson, D. R., & Nevin, J. R. (1975). Determinants of young marrieds' life insurance purchasing behavior: An empirical investigation. *Journal of Risk and Insurance, 42*, 375–388. https://doi.org/10.2307/251694.

Babbel, D. F. (1985). The price elasticity of demand for whole life insurance. *Journal of Finance, 40*(1), 225–239. https://doi.org/10.1111/j.1540-6261.1985.tb04946.x.

Becker, G. S. (1962). Investment in human capital: A theoretical analysis. *Journal of Political Economy, 70*, 9–49. https://doi.org/10.1086/258724.

Berekson, L. L. (1972). Birth order, anxiety, affiliation and the purchase of life insurance. *Journal of Risk and Insurance, 39*, 93–108.

Berkovitch, E., & Venezia, I. (1992). Term vs. whole life insurance—A note. *Journal of Accounting, Auditing & Finance, 7*(2), 214–249.

Burnett, J. J., & Palmer, B. A. (1984). Examining life insurance ownership through demographic and psychographic characteristics. *Journal of Risk and Insurance, 51*(3), 453–467.

Black, K., & Skipper, H. D. (2000). *Life & health insurance* (13th ed.). Upper Saddle River, N.J.: Prentice Hall.

Brenner, T. (Ed.). (1999). *Computational techniques for modeling learning in economics.* Norwell, MA: Kluwer Academic Publishers.

Brock, W. A. (1996). Pathways to randomness in the economy: Emergent non-linearity and chaos in economics and finance. In D. W. Davis (Ed.), *Chaos theory in economics: Methods, models and evidence* (pp. 3–55). Brookfield, VT: Edward Edgar.

Browne, M. J., & Kim, K. (1993). An international analysis of life insurance demand. *Journal of Risk and Insurance, 60*(4), 616–634. https://doi.org/10.2307/253382.

Casti, J. (1992). *Reality rules.* New York, NY: Wiley.

Chen, R., Wong, K. A., & Lee, H. C. (2001). Age, period and cohort effects on life insurance purchases in the U.S. *Journal of Risk and Insurance, 68,* 303–327.

Chesney, M., & Louberge, H. (1986). Risk aversion and the composition of wealth in the demand for full insurance coverage. *Schweizerische Zeitschrift fur Volkswirtschaft und Statistik, 122*(3), 359–370.

Cleeton, D. L., & Zellner, B. B. (1993). Income, risk aversion, and the demand for insurance. *Southern Economic Journal, 60,* 146–156. https://doi.org/10.2307/1059939.

Dechert, W. D. (1996). *Chaos theory in economics: Methods, models, and evidence.* Cheltenham: Edward Elgar.

Duker, J. M. (1969). Expenditures for life insurance among working-wife families. *Journal of Risk and Insurance, 36,* 525–533.

Eisenhauer, J. G., & Halek, M. (1999). Prudence, risk aversion, and the demand for life insurance. *Applied Economic Letters, 6,* 239–242. https://doi.org/10.1080/135048599353429.

Ferber, R., & Lee, L. C. (1980). Acquisition and accumulation of life insurance in early married life. *Journal of Risk and Insurance, 47,* 713–734.

Fischer, S. (1973). A life cycle model of life insurance purchases. *International Economic Review, 14,* 132–152. https://doi.org/10.2307/2526049.

Fitzgerald, J. (1987). The effects of social security on life insurance demand by married couples. *Journal of Risk and Insurance, 54,* 86–99.

Gandolfi, A. S., & Miners, L. (1996). Gender-based differences in life insurance ownership. *Journal of Risk and Insurance, 63,* 683–693.

Goodwin, R. M. (1990). *Chaotic economic dynamics.* New York, NY: Oxford University Press.

Gutter, M. S., & Hatcher, C. B. (2008). Racial differences in the demand for life insurance. *The Journal of Risk and Insurance, 75,* 677–689. https://doi.org/10.1111/j.1539-6975.2008.00279.x.

Halcousis, D. (2005). *Understanding econometrics.* Mason, OH: Thomson South-Western.

Hammond, J. D., Houston, D. B., & Melander, E. R. (1967). Determinants of household life insurance premium expenditure: An empirical investigation. *Journal of Risk and Insurance, 34,* 397–408. https://doi.org/10.2307/250854.

Hau, A. (2000). Liquidity, estate liquidation, charitable motives, and life insurance demand by retired singles. *The Journal of Risk and Insurance, 67*(1), 123–141. https://doi.org/10.2307/253680.

Heo, W., Grable, J. E., & Chatterjee, S. (2013). Life insurance consumption as a function of wealth change. *Financial Services Review, 22*(4), 389–404.

Insurance Information Institute. (2015). *Life insurance.* Retrieved from http://www.iii.org/fact-statistic/life-insurance.

Kovalerchuk, B., & Vityaev, E. (2000). *Data mining in finance.* New York, NY: Springer.

Kwaśnicki, W. (1999). Evolutionary economics and simulation. In T. Brenner (Ed.), *Computational techniques for modeling learning in economics* (pp. 3–44). Norwell, MA: Kluwer Academic.

Lewis, F. D. (1989). Dependents and the demand for life insurance. *American Economic Review, 79*(3), 452–467.

Liebenberg, A. P., Carson, J. M., & Dumm, R. E. (2012). A dynamic analysis of the demand for life insurance. *The Journal of Risk and Insurance, 79,* 619–644. https://doi.org/10.1111/j.1539-6975.2011.01454.x.

Life Insurance Marketing and Research Association. (2014, September). *Facts from LIMRA: Life insurance awareness month.* Retrieved from http://www.limra.com/uploadedFiles/limra.com/LIMRA_Root/Posts/PR/LIAM/PDF/2014-LIAM-Fact-Sheet.pdf.

Lu, C., & Yanagihara, M. (2013). Life insurance, human capital accumulation and economic growth. *Australian Economic Papers, 52,* 52–60. https://doi.org/10.1111/1467-8454.12007.

Lynch, T. (2010). Loss after life. *Journal of Financial Service Professionals, 64*(2), 29–31.

Mantis, G., & Farmer, R. N. (1968). Demand for life insurance. *Journal of Risk and Insurance, 35,* 247–256. https://doi.org/10.2307/250834.

Pines, D. (1988). The economy as an evolving complex system: An introduction to the workshop. In P. Anderson, K. Arrow, & D. Pindes (Eds.), *The economy as an evolving complex system: The proceedings of the evolutionary paths of the global economy workshop, held September, 1987, in Sante Fe, New Mexico* (pp. 3–6). Reading, MA: Addison-Wesley.

Rejda, G. E. (2008). *Principles of risk management and insurance* (10th ed.). Boston, MA: Pearson and Addison Wesley.

Schultz, T. W. (1961). Investment in human capital. *The American Economic Review, 51*(1), 1–17.

Showers, V. E., & Shotick, J. A. (1994). The effects of household characteristics on demand for insurance: A tobit analysis. *The Journal of Risk and Insurance, 61,* 492–502. https://doi.org/10.2307/253572.

Thoyts, R. (2010). *Insurance theory and practice.* New York: Routledge.

Williams, C. A. (1986). Higher interest rates, longer lifetimes, and the demand for life annuities. *Journal of Risk & Insurance, 53,* 164–171. https://doi.org/10.2307/252274.

Xiao, J. J. (1996). Effects of family income and life cycle stages on financial asset ownership. *Journal of Financial Counseling and Planning, 7*(1), 21–30.

Zietz, E. N. (2003). An examination of the demand for life insurance. *Risk Management and Insurance Review, 6,* 159–191. https://doi.org/10.1046/J.1098-1616.2003.030.x.

CHAPTER 2

# Theoretical Background: A New Theoretical Framework for Financial Planning with the Case of Life Insurance Demand—Dynamic Ecological Systemic Framework

**Abstract** This chapter introduces a conceptual and theoretical framework for understanding the behavioral demand for financial planning, specifically for life insurance. The basic background theories of this new framework are introduced and explained. Supporting these theories, the behavioral demand will be distinguished from the classic demand in economics as the term demand in economics has a different meaning depending on behavioral demand. The theories explained in this chapter are ecological systemic theory of family financial management, transformative consumer research, and chaotic dynamics in economics.

**Keywords** Ecological systemic theory · Transformative consumer research · Nonlinear sciences · Dynamic nonlinear systemic approach · Artificial neural network

This chapter and Chapter 3 are two pillars to understand the next chapters. This chapter as the first pillar explains the conceptual and theoretical approach focusing on the main framework of the study, dynamic nonlinear systemic approach. Therefore, in This chapter, foundational theories such as ecological systemic theory, transformative consumer research, and nonlinear sciences are introduced. However, in Chapter 3, there will be general understanding of insurance and the life insurance. For instance, the foundational explanation about risk, risk management, insurance concept, and life insurance will be discussed in Chapter 3.

© The Author(s) 2020
W. Heo, *The Demand for Life Insurance*,
https://doi.org/10.1007/978-3-030-36903-3_2

## 2.1 Introduction to Conceptual and Theoretical Framework

As introduced in the statement of the problem and the purpose of study, a new framework is needed to predict life insurance demand using interdependent interactions among determinants, as an alternative to relying solely on actuarial science and lifespan-related economic approaches. Since the purpose of this research is to improve the prediction of life insurance demand, this study employs a more appropriate framework fitted to the research purpose. This is the dynamic nonlinear systemic framework to predict life insurance demand.

The framework's name comes from natural science research. There have been a few relevant related concepts in the fields of family resource management, marketing, and public policy, as well as among economists, related to nonlinear science and chaotic dynamics. To better understand and explain the framework for this study, two previous frameworks similar to the dynamic nonlinear systemic framework will be described. Next, an explanation will illustrate the conceptual effectiveness of this dynamic nonlinear systemic framework.

### 2.1.1 *Ecological Framework*

Deacon and Firebaugh (1988) introduced a framework for managing family resources. In terms of managing financial resources, managerial behavior and decision-making are thought to be directly associated with purchasing life insurance. The Deacon and Firebaugh framework is an ecological framework that attempts to understand family resource management. Specifically, Deacon and Firebaugh provided a systemic perspective to understand individual and family behaviors. They described the diverse factors that surround individuals and families that influence family resource managerial behaviors, including risk management. The various factors they described are classified as one of three systems: (a) personal system, (b) family system, and (c) ecological system.

The first system, the personal system, exists for each individual. The personal system contains four major stages: (a) input, (b) throughput, (c) output, and (d) feedback (Deacon & Firebaugh, 1988). Throughput is a conceptualization of actual managerial behavior, such as planning and implementing. The remaining three stages are associated with throughput actions. First, during the input stage, many factors influence the throughput. For instance, external demands, internal demands, external resources, and internal resources are expected to influence the throughput. In specific terms, these are family values, family goals, family claims, social norms, social claims, social events, personal goal orientations, family supports, social supports, personal capabilities, personal qualities, life experiences, and relationships. Second, throughput is actual managerial behavior, such as planning and implementing. It contains two features: developing capacities and evolving values. Developing capacities are an individual's cognitive, emotional, social, and physical features. Evolving values are an individual's intrinsic and extrinsic values. Third, by planning and implementing, individuals experience managerial results called "output of the system." The final stage, feedback, is not the same as output. Based on evaluations of an output, an individual can undertake diverse strategies that results in feedback to one's managerial behaviors. As a result, feedback is a proactive reaction after evaluating an output. For example, maintaining management processes, adjusting management, fixing problems, and dropping an approach are possible strategies for individuals to take as feedback.

The second system—the family system—exists for each family. In the case of the family system, most of the features and factors share similarities with the personal system. The family system is an extended version of the personal system. Therefore, the structure (i.e., input, throughput, output, and feedback) with specific features is the same for both systems. However, the difference between the individual and family system is that the individual system is a subsystem of the family system. In the case of the personal system, each individual inside a family is a decision maker in charge of their individual behavior.

However, in the family system, an individual does not make household decisions alone. There is another critical factor among family members—interpersonal communication for decision-making. The existence of interpersonal communication is the differentiation feature between personal and family systems. Deacon and Firebaugh (1988) classified interpersonal communication into three intra-system dynamics: (a) cohesion, (b) adaptability, and (c) functionality. Cohesion denotes the emotional bonding among family members. Adaptability is the changeability of power structure, role, and rule in a family. Functionality is the ability to determine how the family members use human and material resources in the family. As a result, the personal system belongs to the family system and both interact with each other in interpersonal communications.

For both the personal and family systems, feedback takes on a critical role in interpersonal communications. Since positive or negative feedback is given to family members, each person inside a family communicates proactively and decides to retain or change their managerial behaviors as an appropriate strategy. Generally, negative feedback becomes a critical reason for changing managerial behaviors within personal and family systems (Deacon & Firebaugh, 1988). Since positive feedback confirming strategies and behaviors for family resource management are appropriate, a family does not need to change managerial behaviors. However, negative feedback denotes that a family must take another strategy. Thus, negative feedback often leads to a change in managerial strategies and behaviors. Therefore, an experience of negative events could be a factor for employing a managerial behavior.

The third system Deacon and Firebaugh (1988) introduced—ecological system—is defined as "the totality of organisms and environments that interact interdependently" (p. 28). As the definition denotes, outer systems surround the family system. These are known as the macroenvironmental and microenvironmental systems. Deacon and Firebaugh explained that the family system interacts interdependently with macroenvironments and microenvironments.

Macroenvironments consist of two major systems: (a) the natural system and (b) the societal system. The natural system is the physical and biological background associated with societal macroenvironments. For instance, environmental concerns, energy consumption, household waste, weather, and climate are considered to be representative of natural macroenvironments. A natural macroenvironmental system is expected to influence both societies (i.e., local community and families inside a community) with broadly influencing effects. The societal system is a critical system where families survive with other families. This system includes sociocultural, political, economic, and technological environments. The societal structure (e.g., local and religious communities) consists of members, such as individuals and families, and interacts with members inside it. In addition, every individual and family interacts with others inside the same societal system. Therefore, the societal system has a feature of changeability inside the system, as well as a feature of influential effect on each member's managerial behaviors. Furthermore, the societal system interacts with the natural system.

Besides macroenvironments around families, there is a microenvironments system. For instance, physical habitats (e.g., housing status and job-related environments) and social aspects (e.g., neighbors and friends) belong to the microenvironmental system. Deacon and Firebaugh (1988) explained that the microenvironment has a feature of direct propinquity to the family system.

Deacon and Firebaugh (1988) noted that both macroenvironmental and microenvironmental systems interact interdependently of each other, as well as interacting with the family system. Therefore, they named the total system, where sub-systems interdependently interact, as the ecological system. The explanation by Deacon and Firebaugh implies that many influential factors surrounding families likely affect financial decisions interdependently.

Because of interactions among systems, families receive diverse types of feedback. Based on these types of feedback, families may change or retain managerial strategies. Generally, healthy families show a flexibility of adopting changes for better management. Deacon and Firebaugh (1988) named this flexible family system as the morphogenic system. Alternatively, there could be families that do not like to change or are unable to change their system.

Deacon and Firebaugh (1988) indicated the family system is a morphostatic system and further explained that it is possible to link with another field's perspectives. Consider transformative consumer research as combined within marketing and public policy areas.

### 2.1.2 *Transformative Consumer Research*

There is growing academic movement to consider consumer behaviors using contextual and proactive perspectives. Generally, many theories in the social and economic fields of inquiry assume consumers have relatively consistent preferences. For instance, two consumers with the same age and income are expected to show similar consumption tendencies. In other words, there is an assumption of consistency in consumers' states, including behaviors. However, a group of researchers in the Association of Consumer Research have advocated the position that consumers' states are not consistent (Mick, Pettigrew, Pechmann, & Ozanne, 2012). This academic group has changed perceptions of consumers' states from a static viewpoint to a contextual perspective. This perspective is called transformative consumer research (TCR).

From the perspective of TCR, social structure and consumers' behaviors are transformative (Mick et al., 2012). This means social structure and consumer behaviors can be changed by diverse factors on a continuous basis. The changeability of consumer behavior by diverse factors is strongly relevant to the previously presented ecological framework. TCR defines changeability of consumer behavior as the transformative feature of the consumer inside a social context (p. 7). For this reason, TCR researchers tend to have a contextual perspective. Mick et al. explained that TCR highlights the sociocultural context or situational embedding of situations.

For example, regarding life insurance as a precaution for possible future financial vulnerability, TCR researchers might change the definition of consumer vulnerability based on consumers' transformative features. Baker, Gentry, and Rittenburg (2005) redefined consumer vulnerability from a traditional perspective to a new definition that is transformative. Previously, consumer vulnerability was defined by demographic, environmental, and situational factors. For example, past researchers (e.g., Andreasen, 1975; Bankoff, 2001; Gentry, Kennedy, Paul, & Hill, 1995; Kaufman-Scarborough, 1999) defined vulnerable consumers as people with fixed features (e.g., low income, people with chronic disease, people who live in hazardous rural areas, a person who has car accidents, and a family who loses the breadwinner). However, this perspective has limitations related to defining different types of vulnerable consumers, such as mentally challenged consumers. Therefore, Baker et al. suggested a definition of vulnerability as a broad concept in a social context. Diverse factors work as influential elements for vulnerable situations in the consumer context. Individual characteristics (e.g., biophysical and psychological factors) and individual states (e.g., motivation and grief) could affect consumer vulnerability. In addition, external conditions, such as social discrimination and stigmatization, could affect consumer vulnerability. In essence, vulnerability moves away from categories of membership to being defined by the context of a situation.

Another example from TCR is the process theory of consumer vulnerability and resilience. Based on the concept of consumer vulnerability, Baker and Mason (2012) suggested a process theory for consumer vulnerability and resilience. This theory argues that consumers' situations are transformative from vulnerable to resilient situations or from reliable to vulnerable situations. For instance, in the case of moving from a reliable to vulnerable situation, the change occurs through a systemic context. In the occurrence of trigging an event, like the sudden death of the breadwinner, macro-forces (e.g., natural environment, social structure, and regulations) and microenvironments (e.g., family structure and psychological status) could encompass the systemic context where consumers become vulnerable. Harsh living environments, absence of governmental policies, aggressive neighbors, lack of family resources, and low self-efficacy of a person are macro-forces and microenvironments that make consumers vulnerable. In summary, all contexts surrounding a family are possible interactive triggers that can work to make consumers vulnerable. Similarly, contextual interactions among government, companies, individuals, and non-governmental organizations (NGOs) help vulnerable consumers recover to a healthy status. This is strongly linked with the ecological framework suggested by Deacon and Firebaugh (1988).

Shown in the consumer vulnerability example, TCR is strongly relevant to the ecological framework suggested by Deacon and Firebaugh (1988). The different point between these two frameworks is the viewpoint on consumer behavior. The ecological framework, suggested by Deacon and Firebaugh, focuses on better performance in terms of family resource management. TCR focuses on understanding the transformations of consumer behaviors. However, both perspectives have a strong relevance in explaining that consumer behaviors are influenced by diverse factors, including macroenvironments, microenvironments, family features, and individual features. In addition, both perspectives support the notion that multiple factors interdependently interact and influence consumer behaviors.

### *2.1.3 Nonlinear Science in Economic Areas*

As explained in the ecological framework and TCR, many consumer behaviors, including purchasing life insurance, are generally influenced by interactions among diverse factors. In addition, consumer behaviors are not fixed, but changeable. Both interdependent interactions among factors and changeability in consumer behavior are possible in reality. Purchasing life insurance is possibly explained by the concept of complexity.

#### *2.1.3.1 Complexity in the Actual World and Nonlinear Science with Chaotic Dynamics*

The original conceptualization of complexity comes from the natural sciences (i.e., epidemiology, biology, and ecology), since there are many complex phenomena in nature (e.g., weather, earthquakes, and disease). To understand and explain complex phenomena in the natural sciences, it is difficult to identify a specific factor that causes a phenomenon. Normally, many variables work as confounding factors. Because of the complexity of the actual world, researchers in the natural sciences tend to be skeptical about the use of general linearization methods. Generally, the linearization method assumes each specific independent factor is associated with a phenomenon linearly with a specific effect. But a linear association and specific effect are sometimes not observed in the actual world (Brock, 1996a). According to Brock, the tendency to doubt the linearization method gained momentum in the 1980s. Since the 1990s, nonlinear science, which includes the concept of chaos and fractals, has advanced research design dramatically in diverse fields (Casti, 1992).

In addition, doubts about linearization methods, there have been outstanding breakthroughs in computational techniques that make complex analysis possible (Hand, Mannila, & Smyth, 2001; Kudyba, 2014; Linoff & Berry, 2011; Ye, 2014). Specifically, a major reason for using linearization was computational cost. Computational methods have dramatically improved, and the computational costs associated with nonlinear science have decreased enormously. Consequently, there is no reason to rely solely on linearization in the natural sciences. The usefulness of nonlinear science is now known to be a strong alternative way to understand complexity in the social and human fractal world as well. Brock (1996a) explained the reason for using nonlinear science as, "suggestive of pathways to complex dynamics" (p. 9).

Nonlinear science seeks to understand complexity in the actual world through chaotic dynamics (Dechert, 1996; Pines, 1988). Historically, in the natural sciences, Lorenz (1963) introduced the early concept of complexity, specifically in atmospheric science. This is the so-called Lorenz attractor—one of the main theorems within chaos theory. Using the concept of the Lorenz attractor, a structure of nature has a holistic deterministic rule, but many alterations exist inside the structure randomly and stochastically; therefore, randomly occurring alterations are problematic features to analyze and generalize in academia. To solve the analytic problem, fractal structures have been suggested as an additional concept for understanding complexity in complex systems. Fractal structure, another theorem within chaos theory, is strongly associated with the Lorenz attractor (Tél & Gruiz, 2006). Fractal structure means the infinite resemblances between large dynamics and small dynamics. The strong association between chaotic dynamics and a fractal structure denotes that chaotic dynamics have a large dynamic and complex structure. Inside the complex structure, the structure resembles alterations randomly. As a result, to understand complexity in the actual world, chaotic dynamics can be used as a broad conceptual platform for understanding consumer behavior.

Two core hypotheses emerge from chaotic dynamics studies. First, there is a deterministic rule for a holistic structure. Second, inside this holistic structure, there are many alterations occurring through interdependent interactions among numerous factors. These two core axioms seem to resemble the conceptual understanding of reality that follow from the ecological framework and TCR. Applying chaotic dynamics, by using nonlinear science in the natural science, is reasonable in the social and economic sciences. Many researchers (e.g., Barnett et al., 2004; Benhabib, 1992; Brenner, 1999; Goodwin, 1990; Medio, 1992; Morishima, 1980) agree that adopting nonlinear science approaches to understand chaotic dynamics in the social and economic fields is a worthwhile endeavor.

#### *2.1.3.2 Adopting Nonlinear Science in Economics*

Generally, economists seek to discover optimal equilibrium in a market by way of general equilibrium theory. Nonlinear science economists argue the general equilibrium theory in economics has a limitation related to understanding actual complex world scenarios (Anderson, Arrow, & Pines, 1988; Goodwin, 1990; Morishima, 1980; Woodford, 1992). If the situation of an actual economic system is an ideal state (e.g., free competition market), then the general equilibrium theory is able to explain the economic phenomena perfectly. Additionally, the general equilibrium theory works well to explain a market at a given moment. However, reality often shows many fluctuations concurrently and longitudinally. In addition, data also reflect many changes from a long-term perspective.

To solve the problem of fluctuations in time, a few economic trials have been conducted to include oscillatory and fluctuating factors in economic models, such as intertemporal equilibrium and disequilibrium dynamics. Some debates have occurred about these trials to determine whether the trials were empirically valid (Medio, 1992). Debate was caused by an original limitation of stationary attributes of equilibrium in economics. However, the trials in economics provide an important lesson. An alternative method is needed to consider fluctuating and oscillatory events in the social sciences. As a result, Medio (1992) suggested adopting nonlinear science to understand chaotic dynamics in practice, as an alternative method when analyzing fluctuations in economic phenomenon.

Nonlinear science economic equilibrium is different from equilibrium from the perspective of traditional economics. The difference between nonlinear science and traditional economic equilibrium is stability of equilibrium (Medio, 1992). In terms of nonlinear science, equilibrium can be unstable. However, the instability of equilibrium in nonlinear science does not mean a collapse of the entire economic model or system. It means an intrinsic stochasticity inside the whole economic system. As a result, employing nonlinear science in economics means not only an adoption of new methodological tools, but also advances of deductive theories about fluctuations (Medio).

In addition to the equilibrium issue, a major philosophical assumption in classical economics is methodological individualism (Herreiner, 1999). This is basically the same thing as a linear assumption. General economics assumes every economic phenomenon occurs based on an individual person, agent, or market. To explain many phenomena with a simplified, generalized equilibrium formula, methodological individualism ignores the possibility of interdependent interactions among persons, agents, markets, and even macroenvironmental factors. However, in reality, every single person, agent, and market are all interrelated, as shown in previous ecological frameworks and transformative consumer research. Therefore, in order to bring about a better prediction of reality, interdependent interaction must be considered in a conceptual framework.

Furthermore, in economics, one of the major reasons to adopt nonlinear science is random or stochastic events produced by deterministic chaotic dynamics (Farmer & Sidorowich, 1988). Farmer and Sidorowich explained that randomness is mainly caused by ignorance about holistic patterns. For instance, few people can consistently predict where a ball will go in a fair roulette game. This is caused by ignorance of holistic patterns in a roulette game. However, a skilled person (e.g., a professional gambler) may be able to predict where the ball goes because a skilled and observant person has more experience to predict the holistic pattern in a game (Bass, 1985; Thorp, 1985). Farmer and Sidorowich's explanation about ignorance of randomness is directly linked with Brock's (1996a) previous explanation about nonlinear science to understand chaotic dynamics. Bath and Thorp explained chaotic dynamics as follows: The holistic system has a deterministic feature and pattern, but alterations inside the structure have stochastic features.

Based on an understanding of chaotic dynamics, it is possible to adopt nonlinear science to the fields of economics and finance (Farmer & Sidorowich, 1988; Kovalerchuk & Vityaev, 2000). Specifically, adopting nonlinear science methods is expected to improve predictions of behavior. Since traditional economics and finance methodologies focus on finding equilibrium in markets, as explained previously, the purpose of using linearity, as a method, is different from predicting and forecasting the market. Difficulty forecasting in the economics and finance fields is often caused by the complexity of real markets (Kovalerchuk & Vityaev). To solve this forecasting problem, nonlinear science provides a way to understand chaotic dynamics to investigate the association between past data and future values.

#### *2.1.3.3 Examples of Adopting Nonlinear Science in Economic-Related Areas*

A group of scholars at the Santa Fe Institute were among the first to adopt nonlinear science to understand chaotic dynamics in economics. They were interested in merging traditional academics with computer science. Specifically, in terms of merging economics with chaotic dynamics, they initially looked at three topics: (a) cycles, (b) webs, and (c) patterns (Pines, 1988). Cycles denotes "predictive theories of dynamic behavior" (p. 5); webs means "theories of large numbers of interacting units with evolution as the paradigm" (p. 5); and patterns is "theories of inhomogeneity and of self-maintaining differences" (p. 5). The initial attempts at an interdisciplinary investigation with economics and nonlinear science contributed to the enlargement of economics applications in the actual world.

In addition, Arthur (1988) suggested a possible presence of self-reinforcing or autocatalytic mechanisms in economics that limit predictive models. Self-reinforcing (or autocatalytic) means the initial state combined with fluctuations could transform dynamics into an asymptotic state. Using Arthur's explanation, it could be possible to see a self-reinforcing mechanism in a fluctuated economic market, like increasing returns, cumulative causation, and virtuous and vicious circles. This self-reinforcing mechanism in fluctuated economics implies the existence of a dynamic, but predictable, system with fluctuating and random events. Using macroeconomics data, such as quarterly time series industrial production and unemployment rates, Brock (1988) showed an empirical possibility of chaotic dynamics in economics. By utilizing stock return data, Brock extended the empirical possibility of chaotic dynamics to the field of finance.

Besides the effort to adopt nonlinear science to understand chaotic dynamics with actual economic phenomena, a new group who emerged adopted nonlinear science with an evolutionary perspective in economics. Kwaśnicki (1999) named this group evolutionary economists. The name is derived from the fact that economic systems are changeable by diverse factors. Similar to biology, there are evolutions in economics. Evolutionary economists assume the economic system is always changing, similar to the process of evolution. Therefore, the influential factors in the economy also are changing through systemic alterations. This conclusion is strongly associated with the ecological approach suggested by Deacon and Firebaugh (1988) and TCR.

Furthermore, nonlinear science has been adopted in the business field. Burns and Mitchell (1946) suggested that sequential fluctuating changes in economics are possible, which they called the business cycle. They defined the business cycle as a type of fluctuation occurring as a result of recurrent sequential changes in terms of aggregate economic activities. They indicated the business cycle was not only periodic in sequential change, but also recurrent in sequential change. This is similar to Lorenz's (1963) findings in natural science. The entire system has a set of deterministic rules, but diverse events in the whole system could occur stochastically.

Based on Burns and Mitchell's (1946) work, Medio (1992) brought up the possibility that an ordinary equation in economics could not adequately explain a business cycle. Normally, ordinary economic equations are utilized to explain stationary economic phenomena regardless of short-run and long-run dynamics. In other words, ordinary economic equations attempt to simplify the explanation of economic phenomena. However, general economic equations cannot fully explain cyclical fluctuations in business cycles, since these models explain economic phenomena at a specific moment instead of through a time series.

By indicating the atemporal attribute of general economic equations, Medio indicated that general competitive equilibrium is linked to explaining cyclical fluctuations. As a result, to explain sequential fluctuated changes, an alternative academic approach should be employed. Medio suggested nonlinear science methods as such an alternative approach.

As a result, many researchers have adopted dynamic nonlinear methodologies in the field of economics (e.g., Anderson et al., 1988; Benhabib, 1992; Brock, 1988). The reason to adopt nonlinear science is twofold. First, forecasters must deal with many fluctuations and dynamic randomness. Second, the research purpose underlying nonlinear science and other disciplines is different. Researchers who adopt nonlinear science methodologies have a unified purpose of predicting and forecasting phenomena rather than finding a static equilibrium in the market. For instance, Bosarge (1993) used an artificial neural network to improve predictions for the S&P 500, Crude Oil, Yen/Dollar, Eurodollar, and Nikkei indexes. Other researchers (e.g., Refens, Zapranis, & Francis, 1994; Tsibouris & Zeidenberg, 1995) also have noted support for the usefulness of adopting nonlinear science for predictions.

#### *2.1.3.4 Summary*

Nonlinear science can be described by five features. First, there are diverse systemic structures involved with many factors that are assumed to be related to the demand for life insurance. For instance, there are at least three types of systemic structure around a consumer: household-level system, microenvironmental system, and macroenvironmental system. The household-level characteristics will be explained as the smallest systemic structure that includes gender, ethnic background, income, assets, health-related activities, etc. As a midsize structure, microenvironmental system includes job stability, housing status, mobility, religious activities, etc. Macroenvironmental system includes inflation rate, unemployment rate, etc., which will be explained in Chapters 4 and 5. Second, there is a deterministic rule in a systemic structure. In each system, the factors are assumed to be associated with the demand for life insurance as a deterministic rule. Third, a plethora of factors inside the systemic structures interdependently interact with the intra- and inter-structures. For instance, job stability from microenvironmental system may be associated with income from household-level system and unemployment level from macroenvironmental system. Fourth, many alterations exist in actual phenomena because of the third feature. Fifth, alterations are still predictable because alterations occur due to probability and resemble the holistic system. Based on these five features, it is possible to adopt nonlinear science methods to the field of economics, finance, and financial planning. As a result, it is likely possible to adopt nonlinear science to understand and predict the demand for life insurance.

### *2.1.4 Concept of Dynamic Nonlinear Systemic Framework Concepts*

The overarching conceptualization for this study is the dynamic nonlinear systemic framework. The framework is based on the ecological framework, TCR, and adoption of nonlinear science methods. This conceptual framework is used to understand and predict consumer behavior. Specifically, one specific consumer behavior—life insurance demand—is the main focus of this study.

There are two assumptions underlying the use of the framework for this study. First, from the conceptual explanation about family resource management, suggested by Deacon and Firebaugh (1988), the framework for this study employs the concept of a system. The concept of systems is closely aligned with nonlinear modeling (Anderson et al., 1988; Dechert, 1996; Medio, 1992). Specifically, both approaches introduce the concept of systems with a holistic structure and with deterministic rules. Therefore, the first assumption is that, in practice, there are holistic systems directed by deterministic rules.

Second, this study assumes that social and economic phenomena, including consumer life insurance behavior, are changeable and transformative. This assumption comes from both TCR and nonlinear science applications. The changeable and transformative feature is caused by the fact that diverse influential factors interdependently interact with each other at both the intra- and inter-system levels, as shown in Fig. 2.1. To express the changeable and transformative features of social and economic phenomena, this study employs the term dynamic nonlinearity as the name for the model conceptualization. That is, the main framework for this study is referred to as the dynamic nonlinear systemic framework.

As shown in Fig. 2.1, possible influential factors are divided into three systems: a system including household-level factors and two systems comprising out-of-household-level factors. This classification is based on Deacon and Firebaugh's (1988) taxonomy of systems. The original

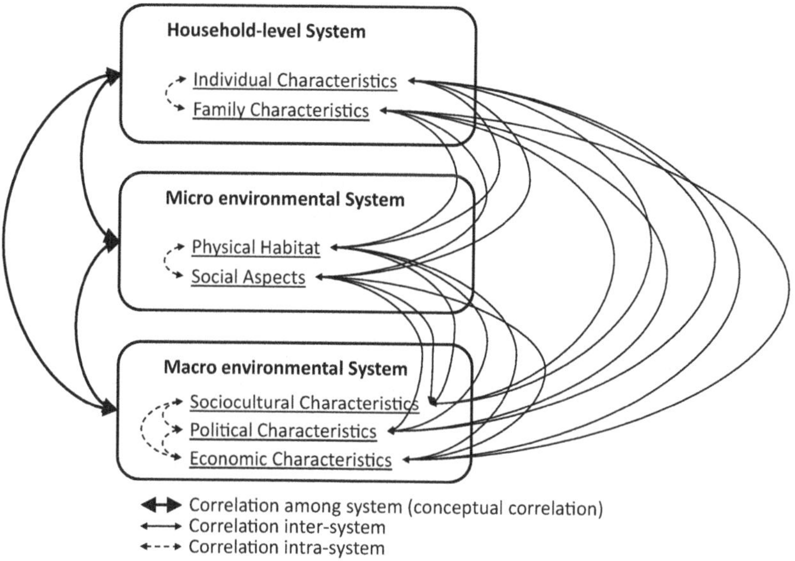


**Fig. 2.1** Example of intra- and inter-system interdependent interactions

classification suggested by Deacon and Firebaugh consisted of a personal system, family system, and ecological system; the ecological system was divided into two sub-systems containing a microenvironmental system and macroenvironmental system. Since the household is the major unit of analysis in this study, the framework merges the personal system and family system into one component that includes household-level factors. From the ecological system, this study employs two sub-systems (i.e., microenvironmental system and macroenvironmental system) as two external factor groups out of the household. A detailed explanation about the empirical factors in each system will be presented and explained in Chapter 3 when discussing the literature.

Each system is conceptually assumed to be correlated with the other systems (bold arrows in Fig. 2.1). For example, diverse factors in the same system are expected to be associated with each other interdependently (broken lines in Fig. 2.1; correlations inter-system). For instance, within the macroenvironmental system political issues, such as redistribution of income through social welfare, are assumed to be associated with the unemployment rate and inflation rate. In the case of the household-level system, a chronic disease of a household member (i.e., individual characteristics) is possibly related to family financial resources (i.e., family characteristics). In addition, a factor from a system is considered to be interdependently related to the other factors, regardless of which system the factor belongs (thin lines in Fig. 2.1; correlations intra-system). For instance, human capital (e.g., education) is generally associated with factors in the macroeconomic system, such as the income level of a country. Cultural norms and the religious environment (i.e., sociocultural characteristics within the macroenvironmental system) can be associated with psychological factors (i.e., individual characteristics in the household-level system).

As a result, the main framework of this study—dynamic nonlinear systemic framework—is based on two axioms: (a) There are holistic systems directed by deterministic rules and (b) diverse influential factors interdependently interact with each other at both the intra- and inter-system levels.

### 2.1.5 Conceptual Artificial Neural Network Model Using the Dynamic Nonlinear Systemic Framework

To transition the conceptual framework into an empirical model, this study employed a data mining method. Generally, data mining methods (e.g., statistics, neighborhoods, clustering, decision trees, neural networks, and induction) are used to investigate actual, rather than normative behavior, including prediction of future consumption and for clustering individuals and households in terms of consumer behavior. Using data mining algorithms, it is possible to discover diverse types of data patterns, such as classification patterns, prediction patterns, cluster and association patterns, data reduction patterns, outlier and anomaly patterns, sequential patterns, and temporal patterns (Ye, 2014).

In academic circles associated with social and economic fields, diverse nonlinear science varieties are derived from differential equations as a starting point (Troitzch, 1999). Therefore, higher-level computational techniques are required for investigations. With the development of computational technologies (i.e., artificial intelligence), various types of techniques have been utilized for investigations. Based on the development of computational technologies, many data mining investigations have already been employed in the marketing field (Berson, Smith,

& Thearling, 2000; Giudici, 2003; Linoff & Berry, 2011; Provost & Fawcett, 2013). Among the diverse methodologies used in data mining, this study employs artificial neural networks (ANNs) to understand and predict life insurance demand.

#### *2.1.5.1 Artificial Neural Networks: A Primer*

McCulloch and Pitts introduced the first trial model for using neurons in academics, in 1943 (Baum, 1988). They attempted to employ brain-like circuits that used neuron-like mechanisms in computer science. These neuron-like mechanisms utilized the sequential delivery of information in a whole circuit. Based on developing the concept of sequential neurons by McCulloch and Pitts, Hopfield (1984) explained that neurons are binary variables. All neurons are connected with each other through synaptic weights. Specifically, when connecting each neuron in computer science, Hopfield introduced higher-order layers among a neural network. In other words, he found that there could be more layers, which produce more connections between input and output neurons. The connections work as amplifiers to produce better output, since they connected all neurons among inputs and outputs.

The concept of ANN comes from the field of computer science. In other words, Hopfield's (1984) neural network model was not initiated for economics; however, since being developed, these models have been used widely in multiple disciplines. Resembling neuron systems of the human brain, ANN is a useful model to fit observations for data classification and future-pattern prediction (Berson et al., 2000; Chen, 2001; Giudici, 2003; Hand et al., 2001; Herbrich, Keilbach, Graepel, Bollmann-Sdorra, & Obermayer, 1999; Kudyba & Kwatinetz, 2014; Linoff & Berry, 2011; Mitchell, 1997; Thompson, 2014; Ye, 2014). Specifically, ANN can be used to detect a pattern from a dataset as a first step toward data analysis. Memorizing this detected pattern, ANN is able to predict the pattern from another dataset. Based on the robustness of predicting a pattern from data, Baum (1988) raised the possibility of using ANN as a mechanism to better understand social and economic phenomena. For instance, Kovalerchuk and Vityaev (2000) determined that ANN shows quite a good forecasting level (85%) for describing purchasing, holding, and selling of stocks in the market. In addition, Herbrich et al. (1999) indicated the usefulness of adopting ANN in economics as a way to classify economic agents and to enhance prediction in a time series. The better performance of predictions in time series data comes from the usage of hidden layers.

Hidden layers increase connections between independent factors and dependent phenomena. In other words, a hidden layer is an intermediate station where all factors are interdependently interacting. A hidden layer is the most critical element inside ANN. Traditionally, most economic analyses assume independent variables have an econometric impact on the dependent variable. The coefficients are mostly defined as a direct association between independent factors and dependent phenomena. However, in terms of ANN, there are a few hidden layers between independent factors and dependent phenomena. As already explained, the hidden layer is an intermediate point where all factors interdependently interact. Therefore, the hidden layer amplifies the prediction power of economic models through a basic algorithm such as the one shown below (see also Fig. 2.2).

$$u = \sum_{i=1}^{n} \omega_i \chi_i \tag{2.1}$$

$$y = f(u - \theta) \tag{2.2}$$

where $u$ denotes the activation unit to reach the function ($f$), $\chi_i$ are input variables, and $\omega_i$ is the weight for each variable; $\theta$ is a threshold to activate the function ($f$); the output ($y$) is calculated when the activation unit ($u$) has a number over threshold ($\theta$).

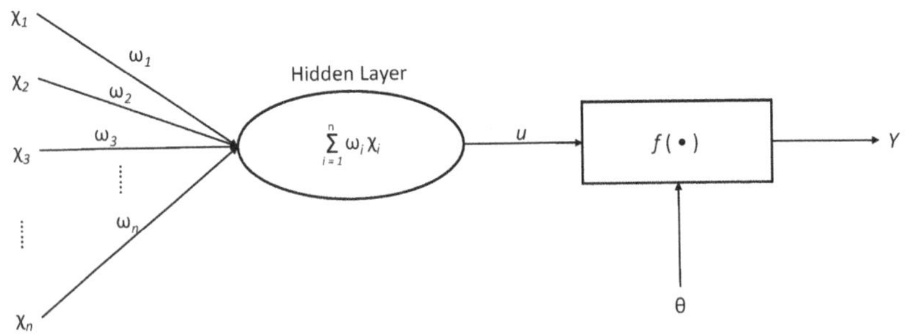


**Fig. 2.2** Basic neuron algorithms

As shown in Fig. 2.2, the hidden layer works as a bridge to link all possible variables to predict social and economic phenomenon. Considering the hidden layer as an intermediate station of variables, ANN is an optimal method for the dynamic nonlinear systemic framework in this study. The reason for using data mining in this study is the critical feature imbedded in nonlinear science that factors are possibly interacting in intra- and inter-systems interdependently. The hidden layer supports a virtual space for factors to interact interdependently.

Considering that a phenomenon is complex (e.g., life insurance purchase behavior), the variables cannot be as simple as Fig. 2.2. As illustrated in Fig. 2.1, variables from diverse systems can have inter- and intra-system correlations. Therefore, the networks have to be changed into multi-layered neural networks. This is shown in Fig. 2.3. As the number of systems increases, the number of hidden layers should also be increased. The number of hidden layers (k) in Fig. 2.3 is optimally determined by the network-finding phase. ANN generally consists of two phases: (a) finding an optimal network from data and (b) predicting a phenomenon with the network. During the first phase, the number of hidden layers (k) is determined. As a result, ANN with hidden layers improves the predictability of the model.

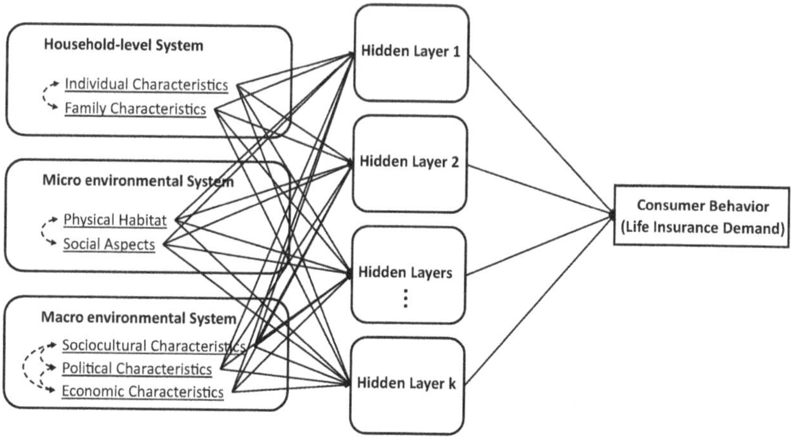


**Fig. 2.3** Artificial neural network algorithms

## 2.2 Definitions

### 2.2.1 *Life Insurance*

Since the research purpose of this study was to predict life insurance demand, a useable life insurance definition is needed. For the purposes of this study, life insurance is defined as: (a) insurance supplied by private insurers, (b) insurance for precaution of death, and (c) insurance products excluding group insurance.

Among the diverse types of insurance products available in the US market, social insurance is distinct from private insurance like life insurance. A distinctive feature between social insurance and private insurance is the assuring object (Black & Skipper, 2000). Social insurance secures social welfare by redistributing total sums of income in the community. For instance, the government gathers financial resources through taxes from all members in the society and redistributes these financial funds to those who need financial support through Social Security, Temporary Assistance for Needy Families, and Supplemental Security Income. However, private insurance secures only personal financial wealth that each individual proactively protects. This study deals only with private insurance demand.

In addition, life insurance is different from other life-associated schemes and products, such as pensions and annuities. Life-associated insurance deals with two types of coverages: loss by death and income uncertainty for a certain length of living time (Black & Skipper, 2000). Specifically, life insurance covers income loss from death, whereas the latter is dealt with by pensions or annuities. However, pensions and annuities focus more on a public purpose, like redistribution of wealth for social welfare (McGill, Brown, Haley, & Schieber, 2005). Therefore, in actual practice, pensions and annuities are purchased with a different intention.

Among diverse types of life insurance (e.g., cash value life insurance, term life insurance, and group life insurance), this study deals with cash value insurance (e.g., whole life insurance). Term life insurance (i.e., pure insurance) does not provide a cash value. Group life insurance is an insurance that covers many people under one contract (Rejda, 2008). Because of this characteristic, group life insurance was not evaluated in the study.

### 2.2.2 *Dynamic Nonlinearity*

Many academic scholars use the concept of dynamic nonlinearity in economic-related fields. Diverse names are used for indicating dynamic nonlinearity, such as chaotic dynamics (Dechert, 1996; Pines, 1988), evolutionary economics (Kwaśnicki, 1999), and nonlinear science or complex system theory (Brock, 1996a).

First, the name chaotic dynamics, suggested by Dechert (1996) and Pines (1988), was introduced as an offshoot of the originality of dynamic nonlinearity. As explained previously, the notion of dynamic nonlinearity came from the natural sciences that investigated the complexity (i.e., chaos) of natural phenomena. Adopting the concept of chaotic dynamics into social and economic phenomena, scholars focused on the concept of nonlinearity and adjusted the name to better match nonlinearity purposes. Specifically, researchers who adopted chaotic dynamics in social and economic fields (e.g., Brock, 1996a; Farmer & Sidorowich, 1988; Medio, 1992) focused on the interdependent correlation among diverse factors that existed in the actual world. In other words, they started to consider nonlinear features among diverse factors. Regardless of the differences among various names, researchers assumed that a large number of variables were all correlated interdependently and had some type of observable pattern.

Based on uniform assumptions, this study unified the method under name of dynamic nonlinearity. As explained previously, the concept of dynamic nonlinearity has five features: (a) existence of diverse systemic structures including influential factors, (b) existence of a deterministic rule in a systemic structure, (c) interdependent correlations among a plethora of factors inside systemic structures, (d) existence of various alterations in actual phenomena, and (e) predictability of alterations by the existence of fractal features. Therefore, in this study, dynamic nonlinearity denotes a feature that a large number of variables from diverse systems have inter- and intra-dependent correlations.

### 2.2.3 *System*

This study adopts the concept of a system from Deacon and Firebaugh's (1988) ecological perspective. According to the original concept suggested by Deacon and Firebaugh, a system consists of four stages:

(a) input, (b) throughput, (c) output, and (e) feedback. Deacon and Firebaugh considered each social structure and environment as systems. Inside a system, each stage has stacks of variables. For instance, individuals are considered to be a personal system. Inside the personal system, diverse variables (e.g., human capital, health status, and psychological features) are interacted within each other. Family is regarded as a larger system. Inside a family system, various variables (e.g., family financial recourse, family structure, and demographic features) are interdependently correlated with each other. In terms of environments, micro- and macroenvironments are all considered as a larger size system. Micro- and macroenvironments comprise many variables (e.g., community characteristics, economic features, and political features) as well. In this study, as all systems comprise many variables, a system means an intangible body that includes several internal variables.

## 2.3 Assumptions and Limitations

This study was premised on two assumptions related to the main framework. First, based on an ecological systemic approach and dynamic nonlinear science, there are holistic systems directed by deterministic rules. Second, based on TCR and nonlinear science applications, changeable and transformative features of life insurance demand are caused by the fact that diverse influential factors interdependently interact with each other at both the intra- and inter-system level.

Since this study employs a dynamic nonlinear systemic framework, there are some methodological limitations associated with this study. As Medio (1992) indicated, there can be a limitation that mathematical dissatisfaction can exist. Specifically, the procedure acts like an unknown function box without a detailed mathematical explanation. As shown in function (2.1), all possible variables are combined with hidden layers. Therefore, it is not easy to know each variable's marginal effect (i.e., coefficient) on life insurance demand. However, the research purpose of this study was not to find the marginal effect provided by each variable. Rather, the research purpose is to improve the prediction of life insurance demand. Even with this limitation, ANN is good tool for predicting demand (Bosarge, 1993; Refens et al., 1994; Tsibouris & Zeidenberg, 1995).

Furthermore, there could be another criticism associated with adopting dynamic nonlinearity in the field of financial planning. The criticism is that nonlinearity is not a critical assumption, since nonlinearity exists as error terms in general linear science methods. Specifically, in terms of macroeconomics and finance, nonlinearity could be considered as a non-statistical error or out-of-sample error, which could occur randomly. However, Brock (1996b) refuted this criticism by showing that the out-of-sample problem could be solved by conditioning detailed information. For instance, LeBaron (1992) improved nonlinear predicting power of the stock market by using local volatility. In other words, by using more detailed data, much of the nonlinearity from random error could be explained by nonlinear science even in economics and finance. Following Brock (1996b) and LeBaron's (1992) advice, this study included possible variables (e.g., inflation rate and unemployment rate) that might contribute to random error. Even though there are a few limitations associated with the use of dynamic nonlinear models, it was deemed an appropriate tool for this study as a way to predict life insurance demand with diverse correlated variables.

Finally, this study was delimited to an analysis of cash value life insurance. This study excludes term insurance. Term insurance has a limited feature for consumer well-being, which is pure precaution of premature death. However, this pure feature of life insurance is not the only factor driving consumers to purchase life insurance. Rather, other additional features of life insurance (i.e., investing and tax savings) also lead consumers to buy life insurance (Black & Skipper, 2000). Varieties of cash value life insurance (e.g., whole life insurance, variable life insurance, universal life insurance, and universal variable life insurance) were not considered in this study.

## 2.4 Summary

Life insurance is an important financial product for households as a precaution for the possible premature death of a household member. Researchers have attempted to understand what factors lead to the demand for life insurance in the market. Generally, actuarial science and lifespan-related theories have been used to guide this type of research. However, research findings based on actuarial science and lifespan-related theories have shown inconsistent findings. The inconsistent results are caused by two factors: (a) unparalleled research purpose with theories and (b) indifference toward interdependent correlations among influential variables. Actuarial science is useful for finding equitable premiums and benefits; lifespan-related theories are worthy for discovering market equilibrium. However, these approaches are less efficient when searching for influential factors of life insurance demand, and they are less proficient when predicting demand for life insurance based on interdependent correlations of diverse influential factors.

To solve the inefficiencies of previously used theoretical frameworks, this study investigates an alternative theoretical framework for better efficiency and prediction of the demand for life insurance. From Deacon and Firebaugh's (1988) ecological system theory, this study employs the concept of system. Systems are intangible bodies that include variables that interact with each other. Based on TCR, this study assumes that consumer behavior, including life insurance purchases, is changeable by interdependent correlations among diverse influential variables. In addition, by adopting dynamic nonlinear science, this study solves the mathematical and methodological issue associated with understanding interdependent correlations among diverse influential variables. As a result, the framework for this study was merged into a dynamic nonlinear systemic framework using the ANN method. By using the dynamic nonlinear systemic framework, this study is better able to explore possible influential variables on the demand for life insurance. Also, this study expects to improve the prediction power among selected influential factors.

## References


Anderson, P. W., Arrow, K. J., & Pines, D. (Eds.). (1988). *The economy as an evolving complex system: The proceedings of the evolutionary paths of the global economy workshop, held September, 1987, in Sante Fe, New Mexico*. Reading, MA: Addison-Wesley.

Andreasen, A. R. (1975). *The disadvantaged consumer*. New York: Free Press.

Arthur, W. B. (1988). Self-reinforcing mechanisms in economics. In P. Anderson, K. Arrow, & D. Pindes (Eds.), *The economy as an evolving complex system: The proceedings of the evolutionary paths of the global economy workshop, held September, 1987, in Sante Fe, New Mexico* (pp. 9–31). Reading, MA: Addison-Wesley.

Baker, S. M., Gentry, J. W., & Rittenburg, T. L. (2005). Building understanding of the domain of consumer vulnerability. *Journal of Macromarketing, 25*, 128–139. https://doi.org/10.1177/0276146705280622.

Baker, S. M., & Mason, M. (2012). Toward a proves theory of consumer vulnerability and resilience: Illuminating its transformative potential. In D. G. Mick,

S. Pettigrew, C. Pechmann, & J. L. Ozanne (Eds.), *Transformative consumer research for personal and collective well being* (pp. 543–563). New York, NY: Routledge.

Bankoff, G. (2001). Rendering the world unsafe: 'Vulnerability' as western discourse. *Disasters, 25,* 19–35. https://doi.org/10.1111/1467-7717.00159.

Barnett, W. A., Gallant, A. R., Hinich, M. J., Jungeilges, J. A., Kaplan, D. T., & Jensen, M. J. (2004). Robustness of nonlinearity and chaos tests to measurement error, inference method, and sample size. In W. Barnett & J. Binner (Eds.), *Contributions to Economic Analysis: Vol. 261. Functional structure and approximation in econometrics* (pp. 529–548). Bingley, UK: Emerald Group Publishing. https://doi.org/10.1108/s0573-8555(2004)0000261030.

Bass, T. (1985). *Eudaemonic Pie.* New York: Houghton Mifflin.

Baum, E. B. (1988). Neural nets for economics. In P. Anderson, K. Arrow, & D. Pindes (Eds.), *The economy as an evolving complex system: The proceedings of the evolutionary paths of the global economy workshop, held September, 1987, in Sante Fe, New Mexico* (pp. 33–48). Reading, MA: Addison-Wesley.

Benhabib, J. (Ed.). (1992). *Cycles and chaos in economic equilibrium.* Princeton, NJ: Princeton University Press.

Berson, A., Smith, S., & Thearling, K. (2000). *Building data mining applications for CRM.* New York, NY: McGraw-Hill.

Black, K., & Skipper, H. D. (2000). *Life & health insurance* (13th ed.). Upper Saddle River, NJ: Prentice Hall.

Bosarge, W. E. (1993). Adaptive processes to exploit the nonlinear structure of financial markets. In R. Trippi & E. Turban (Eds.), *Neural networks in finance and investing* (pp. 371–402). Chicago, IL: Probus.

Brenner, T. (Ed.). (1999). *Computational techniques for modeling learning in economics.* Norwell, MA: Kluwer Academic Publishers.

Brock, W. A. (1988). Nonlinearity and complex dynamics in economics and finance. In P. Anderson, K. Arrow, & D. Pindes (Eds.), *The economy as an evolving complex system: The proceedings of the evolutionary paths of the global economy workshop, held September, 1987, in Sante Fe, New Mexico* (pp. 77–97). Reading, MA: Addison-Wesley.

Brock, W. A. (1996a). Pathways to randomness in the economy: Emergent nonlinearity and chaos in economics and finance. In D. W. Davis (Ed.), *Chaos theory in economics: Methods, models and evidence* (pp. 3–55). Brookfield, VT: Edward Edgar.

Brock, W. A. (1996b). Understanding macroeconomic time series using complex systems theory. In D. W. Davis (Ed.), *Chaos theory in economics: Methods, models and evidence* (pp. 1141–1193). Brookfield, VT: Edward Edgar.

Burns, A. F., & Mitchell, W. C. (1946). *Measuring business cycles.* New York, NY: National Bureau of Economic Research.

Casti, J. (1992). *Reality rules.* New York, NY: Wiley.

Chen, Z. (2001). *Data mining and uncertain reasoning: An integrated approach.* New York, NY: Wiley.

Deacon, R. E., & Firebaugh, F. M. (1988). *Family resource management: Principles and applications* (2nd ed.). Boston, MA: Allyn & Bacon.

Dechert, W. D. (1996). *Chaos theory in economics: Methods, models, and evidence.* Cheltenham: Edward Elgar.

Farmer, J. D., & Sidorowich, J. J. (1988). Can new approach to nonlinear modeling improve economic forecasts? In P. Anderson, K. Arrow, & D. Pindes (Eds.), *The economy as an evolving complex system: The proceedings of the evolutionary paths of the global economy workshop, held September, 1987, in Sante Fe, New Mexico* (pp. 99–115). Reading, MA: Addison-Wesley.

Gentry, J. W., Kennedy, P. F., Paul, K., & Hill, R. P. (1995). The vulnerability of those grieving the death of a loved one: Implications for public policy. *Journal of Public Policy & Marketing, 14,* 128–142. https://doi.org/10.2307/253478.

Giudici, P. (2003). *Applied data mining: Statistical methods for business and industry.* Hoboken, NJ: Wiley.

Goodwin, R. M. (1990). *Chaotic economic dynamics.* New York, NY: Oxford University Press.

Hand, D., Mannila, H., & Smyth, P. (2001). *Principles of data mining.* Cambridge: MIT Press.

Herbrich, R., Keilbach, M., Graepel, T., Bollmann-Sdorra, P., & Obermayer, K. (1999). Neural networks in economics. In T. Brenner (Ed.), *Computational techniques for modeling learning in economics* (pp. 169–196). Norwell, MA: Kluwer Academic Publishers.

Herreiner, D. K. (1999). Local interaction as a model of social interaction. In T. Brenner (Ed.), *Computational techniques for modeling learning in economics* (pp. 221–239). Norwell, MA: Kluwer Academic Publishers.

Hopfield, J. J. (1984). Neurons with graded response have collective properties life those of two-state neurons. *Proceedings of the National Academy of Sciences, USA, 81,* 3088–3092. https://doi.org/10.1073/pnas.81.10.3088.

Kaufman-Scarborough, C. (1999). Reasonable access for mobility-disabled persons is more than widening the door. *Journal of Retailing, 75,* 479–508. https://doi.org/10.1016/S0022-4359(99)00020-2.

Kovalerchuk, B., & Vityaev, E. (2000). *Data mining in finance: Advances in relational and hybrid methods.* Boston, MA: Kluwer Academic Publishers.

Kudyba, S. (Ed.). (2014). *Big data, mining, and analytics.* Boca Raton, FL: CRC Press and Taylor & Francis.

Kudyba, S., & Kwatinetz, M. (2014). Introduction to the big data era. In S. Kudyba (Ed.), *Big data, mining, and analytics* (pp. 1–15). Boca Raton, FL: CRC Press and Taylor & Francis.

Kwaśnicki, W. (1999). Evolutionary economics and simulation. In T. Brenner (Ed.), *Computational techniques for modeling learning in economics* (pp. 3–44). Norwell, MA: Kluwer Academic Publishers.

LeBaron, B. (1992). Some relations between volatility and serial correlation in stock market returns. *Journal of Business, 65,* 199–219. https://doi.org/10.1086/296565.

Linoff, G. S., & Berry, M. J. A. (2011). *Data mining techniques: For marketing, sales, and customer relationship management* (3rd ed.). Indianapolis, IN: Wiley.

Lorenz, E. N. (1963). Deterministic non-periodic flow. *Journal of Atmospheric Science, 20,* 130–141. https://doi.org/10.1175/1520-0469(1963)020<0130:DNF>2.0.CO;2.

McCulloch, W. A., & Pitts, W. (1943). A logical calculus of the ideas immanent in neural nets. *Bulletin of Mathematical Biophysics, 5,* 115–137. https://doi.org/10.1007/BF02478259.

McGill, D. M., Brown, K. N., Haley, J. J., & Schieber, S. J. (2005). *Fundamentals of private pensions.* New York, NY: Oxford University Press.

Medio, A. (1992). *Chaotic dynamics: Theory and applications to economics.* New York, NY: Cambridge University Press.

Mick, D. G., Pettigrew, S., Pechmann, C., & Ozanne, J. L. (Eds.). (2012). *Transformative consumer research for personal and collective well-being.* New York, NY: Taylor & Francis.

Mitchell, T. M. (1997). *Machine learning.* New York, NY: McGraw-Hill.

Morishima, M. (1980). *Dynamic economic theory.* London, UK: International Centre for Economics and Related Disciplines.

Pines, D. (1988). The economy as an evolving complex system: An introduction to the workshop. In P. Anderson, K. Arrow, & D. Pindes (Eds.), *The economy as an evolving complex system: The proceedings of the evolutionary paths of the global economy workshop, held September, 1987, in Sante Fe, New Mexico* (pp. 3–6). Reading, MA: Addison-Wesley.

Provost, F., & Fawcett, T. (2013). *Data science for business.* Sebastopol, CA: O'Reilly Media Inc.

Refens, A. N., Zapranis, A., & Francis, G. (1994). Stock performance modeling using neural networks: A comparative study with regression models. *Neural Networks, 7,* 375–388.

Rejda, G. E. (2008). *Principles of risk management and insurance* (10th ed.). Boston, MA: Pearson/Addison-Wesley.

Tél, T., & Gruiz, M. (2006). *Chaotic dynamics.* New York, NY: Cambridge Press.

Thompson, W. (2014). Data mining methods and the rise of big data. In S. Kudyba (Ed.), *Big data, mining, and analytics* (pp. 71–101). Boca Raton, FL: CRC Press and Taylor & Francis.

Thorp, E. O. (1985). *The mathematics of gambling*. Secaucus, NJ: Lyle Stuart.

Troitzch, K. G. (1999). Simulation as a tool to model stochastic processes in complex systems. In T. Brenner (Ed.), *Computational techniques for modeling learning in economics* (pp. 45–69). Norwell, MA: Kluwer Academic Publishers.

Tsibouris, G., & Zeidenberg, M. (1995). Testing the efficient markets hypotheses with gradient descent algorithms. In A. Refenes (Ed.), *Neural networks in the capital markets* (pp. 127–136). New York, NY: Wiley.

Woodford, M. (1992). Imperfect financial intermediation and complex dynamics. In J. Benhabib (Ed.), *Cycles and chaos in economic equilibrium* (pp. 253–276). Princeton, NJ: Princeton University Press.

Ye, N. (2014). *Data mining: Theories, algorithms, and examples*. Boca Raton, FL: CRC Press and Taylor & Francis Group.

CHAPTER 3

# Literature Review: Previous Literature for Understanding Life Insurance and Behavioral Demand for Life Insurance

**Abstract** In this chapter, a literature review focuses on behavioral demand for life insurance. Basic explanations about risk and risk management are discussed first to explain life insurance, specifically in the realm of personal finance. After understanding the general terminology about risk and risk management, the personal needs of life insurance buyers will be explained in this chapter. All explanations include a review of studies and scholarly works related to the research proposed for this analysis.

**Keywords** Risk · Risk management · Need of insurance · Life insurance

As explained in the first part of Chapter 2, this chapter is another pillar to explain the basic knowledge to understand the life insurance. In previous Chapter 2, there was a conceptual and theoretical explanation focusing on the main theoretical framework of the study, dynamic nonlinear systemic approach. However, in this chapter, there will be general understanding about the insurance and the life insurance. For example, the foundational explanation about risk, risk management, need of insurance, and life insurance will be discussed in this chapter.

© The Author(s) 2020
W. Heo, *The Demand for Life Insurance*,
https://doi.org/10.1007/978-3-030-36903-3_3

## 3.1 Historical Context Discussion

One of the main reasons people need to purchase life insurance is as a precaution for an unexpected event like the premature death of a household breadwinner or a member of a household (Rejda, 2008; Thoyts, 2010). Losing the primary breadwinner of a household critically increases the financial vulnerability of a household, since the major source of income disappears with the death of the wage earner. Even if a person who dies is not a household's breadwinner, the loss of a member of a household can generate various economic burdens on the other members in a household. The premature death of a household member could leave an unpaid medical bill and possible debt to the others of a household (Rejda). This illustrates how life insurance works as a tool for managing the risk of premature death in a household.

This discussion about life insurance begins with a review of family risk management. The first step toward understanding the interrelated complexities among the determinants of life insurance demand involves understanding the purpose of risk management and life insurance. Based on an understanding of risk, risk management, consumers' need for insurance, and life insurance, it is possible to identify the factors that are generally expected to influence the demand for life insurance.

### 3.1.1 *Understanding Risk, Risk Management, and the Need for Insurance*

Insurance is a tool for confronting risk. Specifically, life insurance is a risk management tool. Therefore, the starting point to understanding the use of any type of insurance from a consumer perspective, including life insurance, should start with understanding the concept of risk. Thoyts (2010) defined risk as "the probability of an uncertain event, causative of economic loss" (p. 5). Rejda (2008) defined risk as the "uncertainty concerning the occurrence of a loss" (p. 3). Different from Thoyts' definition, Rejda linked the term of risk with the concept of "chance of loss." Rejda defined chance of loss as "the probability that an event will occur" (p. 4). On the other hand, Thoyts (2010) combined chance of loss and risk broadly. Regardless of how broad or narrow risk is defined, the term for risk always includes uncertainty—a so-called stochastic feature. This is the reason nearly all research studies about risk and insurance consider the probability of events and the stochastic feature for risk.

To solve the stochastic problem of predicting risk, there is a need to identify the existence of risk. Rejda (2008) described the following steps to identify risk. First, people who exposed to a chance of loss should acknowledge the possibility and identify the various areas in which risk can occur, including property, liability, financial, human resources, and others. For instance, those exposed to the chance of loss of human resources ought to detect the possible death of the household breadwinner or possible injury rate of the main wage earner. Second, after detecting the chance of loss, the chance of loss should be analyzed as a way to predict the loss probability. For example, the frequency of injury or average death age of people should be analyzed as a form of human resource risk management. Similarly, Thoyts (2010) detailed five steps to identify risk: (a) risk perception, (b) risk confirmation, (c) risk causation, (d) risk consequences, and (e) hazard factors. Risk perception denotes a person's recognition of a possible risk. Risk confirmation tells whether the recognized risk is harmful or not. Risk causation is the identification of an effect caused by the risk. Risk consequences mean the significant costs associated with the effect. Finally, hazard factors are precursors of risk that increase or decrease the probability and effects of risk.

Identifying the possible existence of risk is a total solution to manage risk. Two additional steps need to be taken: (a) categorizing types of risk and (b) taking appropriate strategies for confronting risk.

First, researchers have used diverse methods to classify risk into specific categories. For instance, Thoyts (2010) categorized risk into four categories, based on a risk's severity: (a) catastrophic, (b) severe, (c) minor, and (d) trivial. Even though these four categories seem simple, the implication is important in terms of risk management. Since each category has a different cost outcome when an actual event occurs, recognition of risk severity is one way to estimate premiums and benefits. For instance, in the case of life insurance, it is critical to anticipate when a breadwinner might die.

Besides categorizing risk by severity, economic risk can be classified by output, effect, and nature (Rejda, 2008; Thoyts, 2010). By output, economic risk is classified as either pure risk or speculative risk. As the terms denote, pure risk contains only loss, whereas speculative risk includes both loss and gain. For instance, death is a pure risk, but gambling is a speculative risk. Based on the effect, economic risk is categorized as either particular or fundamental risk. Particular risk exists on an individual or a small group basis; however, fundamental risk occurs within a large population. For example, the chance of an automobile accident occurring belongs to particular risks. Alternatively, the chance of loss among huge numbers of people resulting from an earthquake is a type of fundamental risk. Finally, economic risk can be classified by nature into static and dynamic risks. Static risk denotes a one-time accident, like a fire or earthquake; a dynamic risk is a changeable risk like a change in law.

Second, after identifying one or more risks, risk needs to be managed by employing appropriate strategies. As described previously, there are a number of diverse strategies to control and manage identified risks. Rejda (2008) suggested five methods, Black and Skipper (2000) described four strategies, and Thoyts (2010) suggested three ways.

Specifically, Rejda (2008) recommended five methods to prepare for a possible loss: (a) avoidance, (b) loss prevention and reduction, (c) retention, (d) noninsurance transfer, and (e) commercial insurance. Avoidance is akin to escaping from risk (e.g., living in a low crime rate area). Loss prevention and reduction involve preventing or lowering risk (e.g., defensive driving on the highway and installing a building sprinkler system). Retention is to concede the management of risk because of the small risk effect. Generally, risk retention occurs when the expected loss is not critical. Without using insurance, noninsurance transfer moves risk from one party to another party. For instance, purchasing a warranty is a type of noninsurance transfer. Commercial insurance involves purchasing insurance.

Black and Skipper (2000) suggested four tools of risk management: (a) risk avoidance, (b) risk reduction, (c) risk transfer, and (d) risk retention. Black and Skipper merged noninsurance transfer and insurance into one category, risk transfer. In terms of Thoyts' categories, Thoyts defined risk control as three types: (a) risk elimination, (b) risk transfer, and (c) risk reduction. Thoyts merged risk avoidance into risk elimination. The critical point linking their strategies (i.e., Rejda; Black and Skipper; and Thoyts) is that regardless of the number of methods, all strategies include risk transfer as a major method used to manage risk. Risk transfer indicates moving financial consequences from one party to another. Life insurance is the key risk transfer product of interest in this study.

Among these risk categorizations and management strategies, not all risks are insurable. Rejda (2008) outlined six requirements for an insurable risk: (a) a number of exposure units, (b) accidental and unintentional loss, (c) determinable and measurable loss, (d) no catastrophic loss, (e) calculable chance of loss, and (f) economically feasible premium. First, there should be a large number of people facing a similar risk. If a risk exists on a specific small group of people, insurers may be unable to actuarially account for the risk because of a high chance of loss. Second, insurance should cover only accidental and unintentional loss. Intentional loss is associated with moral hazard, as well as skewing the statistical randomness of events. Third, losses should be predictable by cause and time. Fourth, catastrophic losses, like those resulting from earthquakes and terrorism, are not easily covered by insurance since insurance basically works as a pooling mechanism. Large numbers of people harmed by a catastrophe at the same time do not have enough collective financial resources to cover the loss. However, there is a need to insure catastrophic losses from a public policy perspective. Therefore, financial instruments have been designed for use in dealing with catastrophic losses, such as reinsurance and catastrophic bonds. Fifth, it should be possible to estimate the average frequency and the average severity of losses. Insurance companies are typically unable to manage their solvency for various losses without estimating the frequency and severity of risks. Finally, insurance should be economically beneficial, to both the insured and the insurer. In summary, insurance for individuals, like life insurance, is associated with pure risk, particular risk, and static risk. These risks can be defined as personal risks.

After identifying risk, and taking appropriate management strategies, the final step is to implement selected methods to manage risk. Although there are diverse risk management methods, as explained above, the human response to risk is a complicated concept to define and measure (Thoyts, 2010). Generally, human responses to risk can be classified into three categories: (a) risk averse, (b) risk neutral, and (c) risk tolerant. It is not possible to divide people perfectly into these three categories. Therefore, the human response to risk is generally measured, based on a scale, with risk averse on one end and risk tolerant on the other. Because of the complexities of measuring human responses toward risk, it is difficult to understand which factors practically influence the use of life insurance. The key point is that risk is the major precondition for the demand on insurance. While managing risk, diverse factors, such as the health of the household breadwinner, psychological variables, and the economic status of a household, correlate with each other and lead to the demand for insurance. Also, it is important to understand how these various factors interact with each other and how these interrelations influence the demand for insurance. After all, it is critically important to consider the complexity of the real world when predicting the demand for life insurance.

### *3.1.2 Personal Need for Life Insurance*

The main purpose of purchasing life insurance is the restoration of lost income due to a breadwinner's death (Rejda, 2008). Essentially, the death benefit can be used to generate cash flows for survivors. Rejda explained that premature death has a different impact on diverse types of family structures (e.g., single people, single-parent families, two-income earners with children families, traditional families, blended families, and sandwiched families). Single individuals generally do not worry about the financial implications of death, since there are no income dependents. However, other families could face critical financial problems in the event of a premature death of a breadwinner, regardless of the family structure. Since most family members are financially dependent on a breadwinner's financial resources (e.g., labor income), the breadwinner's death nearly always results in a severe financial loss.

However, life insurance does not only serve one specific purpose of buffering against premature death of a household breadwinner. Life insurance also serves other purposes in the financial planning process, such as providing tax savings on wealth transfers and allowing for tax-deferred investment of assets. For instance, purchasing a certain form of life insurance, such as second-to-die policies in an irrevocable life insurance trust, is a typical financial planning strategy that results in tax savings on estates, gifts, income, and bequests (Clark, 2010; Cymbal, 2013; Kait 2012; Whitelaw, 2014). In addition, life insurance is one of the key products used by consumers to prepare for retirement (Tannahill, 2012). Furthermore, many researchers and practitioners indicate that life insurance can be used as an investment tool (Cordell & Landgon, 2013). The demand for life insurance not only originates as a response to the possibility of a premature death, but the demand for life insurance is also driven by diverse financial planning and investing needs.

### *3.1.3 Understanding Life Insurance*

Life insurance is just one of a variety of insurance products. There are various perspectives to understanding insurance, including legal, economic, historical, and actuarial. Even though it is difficult to define insurance in a few words, Rejda (2008) adopted a definition from the Commission on Insurance Terminology of the American Risk and Insurance Association in 1965 as follows: "Insurance is the pooling of fortuitous losses by transfer of such risks to insurers, who agree to indemnify benefits on their occurrence, or to render services connected with the risk" (p. 19). Black and Skipper (2000) defined insurance as "a financial intermediation function by which individuals exposed to a specified contingency each contribute to a pool from which covered events suffered by participating individuals are paid" (p. 2). Thoyts (2010) described the two major consumer side functions of insurance as a risk transfer mechanism and a risk-spreading mechanism. A risk transfer mechanism denotes the actual occurrence of moving risk from a policyholder to insurer. In terms of a risk-spreading mechanism, an annual premium is a long-term cost for the possible actual occurrence of risk. In summary, the broad concept of insurance denotes a financial tool that transfers financial risk from individual insureds to a financial gathering pool managed by an insurer.

Specifically, the basic characteristics of insurance are: (a) pooling of losses, (b) payment of fortuitous losses, (c) risk transfer, and (d) indemnification (Rejda, 2008). Pooling of losses denotes sharing a few losses among members in a large group. In other words, insurance consumers pay together, so insurance can pay for a few possible accidental events. Payment for fortuitous losses means insurance should pay only for unintentional losses. Risk transfer occurs when insured people shift their losses to insurers by insurance contracts. Indemnification is the act of financial recovery via insurance.

As explained previously, the primary reason why people need to purchase life insurance is to buffer against financial losses caused by death. Rejda (2008) defined premature death as "the death of a family head with outstanding unfulfilled financial obligations" (p. 211). Under this definition, the loss of children is not included in the concept of premature death. Premature death causes four financial problems: (a) loss of human life value, (b) additional expenses by funeral and unpaid medical bills, (c) confrontation of insufficient future income, and

(d) noneconomic costs including emotional issues. In terms of premature death, the problem is the uncertainty of death. The death of a person is certain, but the timing of death is uncertain (Thoyts, 2010). For this reason, life insurance is needed as a financial planning tool. Thoyts suggested three major reasons for purchasing insurance: (a) risk aversion, (b) legal compulsion, and (c) contractual obligations. Specifically, in terms of life insurance, risk aversion is the main reason why consumers purchase life insurance. Generally, the other two reasons do not lead general consumers (i.e., the public) to purchase life insurance.

In addition to the basic reason for purchasing life insurance, Black and Skipper (2000) indicated several advantages associated with the purchase of life insurance. From a consumer perspective, life insurance is a better option than saving for possible premature death. Thinking about the possibility of death of any household member, savings generally will not be sufficient if the inflation rate is greater than interest rates. Life insurance secures a certain amount of value for confronting a death for those who cannot self-insure losses. Therefore, in terms of confronting a death, life insurance is a better option than savings. Second, life insurance is a relatively safe method of investing by providing a type of savings with cash value. Generally, cash value life insurance policies have a forced savings component that builds value over time. In addition, life insurance is able to build wealth while minimizing tax payments. Third, life insurance creates stability in terms of psychological and emotional well-being. Having life insurance, consumers do not need to worry as much about financial loss caused by the premature death of insured household members.

From a socioeconomic perspective, there are additional advantages for people who purchase life insurance (Black & Skipper, 2000). First, life insurance is able to fill an asset gap that the government is not able to support. Social welfare is unable to support all needs in a society. Therefore, private life insurance is needed to meet lost asset values due to death. Second, life insurance improves the macroeconomic system because private insurers are permitted to invest in the markets, which enhances liquidity. Additionally, as life insurers invest funds in other firms, they are able to provide monitoring of the markets. The monitoring system by insurers leads markets to better transparency and soundness. Investigations about the determinants of the demand for life insurance become more meaningful when viewed from both a personal and macroeconomic perspective.

### 3.1.4 *Understanding Life Insurance Demand: The Actuarial Perspective*

Investigating the determinants of the demand for life insurance requires a knowledge of previously used theoretical models. The first basic theoretical approach used to explain life insurance demand is actuarial science. Actuarial science helps insurers and regulators decide the equitable premium to charge for life insurance. In addition, the mathematical and statistical reasoning behind the actuarial approach helps insurers and regulators set fair benefits for policyholders and their beneficiaries. Premiums and benefits are the "price" of insurance. As such, these variables are important factors influencing the demand for life insurance. Therefore, understanding the actuarial science framework in shaping premiums and benefits is critical to estimating the demand for life insurance.

The root of actuarial science comes from life-associated insurance. During the seventeenth century, mathematicians began estimating life expectancy in response to premature death being a social problem in Britain (Thoyts, 2010). Many breadwinners died before reaching their expected lifespan during the industrialization period in Britain. These premature deaths lowered social welfare because of the loss of the main wage earners' incomes. Life-associated insurance appeared to solve the problem. Mathematicians launched the field of actuarial science in response to predicting life expectancies. For this reason, the first actuarial science studies began by estimating the probability of premature death.

Dynamic changes in the nineteenth century increased the need for life-associated financial products, including pensions, annuities, and life insurance (McGill, Brown, Haley, & Schieber, 2005). Dynamic changes during the nineteenth century in the United States included an increasing population, continuing industrialization, urbanization, increasing longevity, and unemployment problems. Because of these dynamic social and economic changes, people began worrying about losing their jobs, retirement, and premature death. To cope with these worries, the government and private insurance companies in the United States began to supply life-associated financial products. To support the equitable premium of life-associated financial products, actuarial science was widely utilized to estimate the probability of premature death or longevity.

However, it was soon learned that the probability of occurring events, like premature death, is not perfectly predictable. Because of this, insurers utilize special methods to estimate the probability of event occurrence when quoting premiums. The method is to review past outcomes (Thoyts, 2010). The basic theorem used when reviewing the past is the law of large numbers. The more records from the past that are analyzed lead to a more accurate estimation of event probability in the future. Specifically, a large number of records follow the central theorem, so the distribution probability of a large number becomes almost similar to the normal distribution. The central limit theorem and the normal distribution are core concepts embedded in actuarial science (Rejda, 2008; Thoyts, 2010), as well as in investment management (Bodie, Kane, & Marcus, 2010). Based on the normal distribution, it is possible to predict an average chance of loss in risk management or an average rate of return on an investment. With these averages, it is possible to estimate 66.26% or 95.44% of the variance in chance of loss or rate of return. This implies that chance of loss and rate of return are based on probabilities. As a result, based on the statistical approach, on which actuarial science is based, prediction of the probability of premature death seems deterministic. However, since premature death itself is still stochastic, this estimation is not a perfect way of estimation, but rather a sufficient form of estimation.

Because a deterministic statistical approach is not a perfect tool to estimate the probability of a premature death, there is another method used to estimate the probability of premature death when deciding an equitable premium—stochastic modeling. Using stochastic modeling, researchers review many random variables, such as the number of claims, the number of catastrophes, and other economic variables (Thoyts, 2010). Based on many random variables, researchers can determine patterns of occurrence probability. Specifically, insurers in the life insurance industry tend to use stochastic modeling, since life insurance covers, in general, long-term policies (i.e., 10 years or more). To predict the long-term occurrence of events, finding patterns is a more efficient method to estimate equitable premiums compared to simply reviewing the past. Thoyts explained that many life insurers consider investment returns, inflation, interest rates, and mortality rate as major factors for determining patterns.

From a statistical viewpoint, the stochastic feature is an essential tool to estimate the probability of premature death when identifying equitable premiums. Specifically, in actuarial science, stochastic features can be found in a diverse number of analyses. For instance, the classical financial model in actuarial science explains how personal capital is distributed over an individual's lifetime (Vylder, 1997). Vylder defined distributed capital over an individual's lifetime as time capital. The natural feature of time capital is stochastic. Specifically, in terms of life insurance, remaining lifetime is a stochastic factor that impacts time capital, since surviving time is not deterministic. Therefore, time capital naturally includes a stochastic feature. In addition to the concept of time capital, other concepts in actuarial science, such as the concept of mortality, life tables, net premiums, and multiple decrement models, are all functioned by a few simple statistical variables, such as life value, stochastic length of living time, and probability of cancellation (Dickson, Hardy, & Waters, 2013; Kling, 1993; Pitacco, Denuit, Haberman, & Olivieri, 2009; Vylder, 1997).

As previously explained, actuarial science's purpose is to estimate equitable premiums and benefits for insurers and policyholders. Therefore, most variables used in actuarial science are limited to several probabilistic and stochastic factors (e.g., mortality rate, life tables, life value, and life expectancy) for estimating the demand for life insurance. Therefore, actuarial science is a more efficient way to estimate equitable premiums but less efficient as an approach to find influential factors on the demand for life insurance.

### *3.1.5 Understanding Life Insurance Demand: The Lifespan-Related Economics Perspective*

The second basic approach used to understand life insurance is lifespan-related economic theories. From the perspective of lifespan analyses, there are two major economic explanations as to why people need to purchase life insurance: the life cycle hypothesis and human capital theory. First, the life cycle model and permanent income theory explain the rationale of why people need to purchase life insurance (Black & Skipper, 2000). Ando and Modigliani (1963) developed the life cycle model. Diverse literatures support the linkage between the life cycle model and the need for life insurance. Using the life cycle hypothesis, Yaari (1965) offered an economic explanation about the reason why life insurance and annuities are necessary (Lewis, 1989). Yaari utilized the economic demand function, based on the life cycle model, and showed the positive effect on a household's utility by purchasing fair life insurance or fair annuities. In addition, Fischer (1973) used the life cycle model with economic utility functions. Fischer found a financial source for living was associated with the purchase of life insurance. People living on labor income were predicted to purchase life insurance, whereas people living off the proceeds of wealth would not purchase life insurance.

Since the life cycle hypothesis explains how people distribute their income or wealth during the lifespan, Black and Skipper (2000) explained that the hypothesis supports the need for life insurance. Extra income during midlife should theoretically be saved to prepare for retirement or possible premature death. For this reason, life insurance should be purchased based on the hypothesis. In addition, the literature (e.g., Fischer, 1973; Lewis, 1989; Pissarides, 1980; Yaari, 1965) using the life cycle hypothesis has employed an economic demand function based upon the association between price and quantity. In other words, the life cycle hypothesis focuses on the market instead of influential factors for the demand for life insurance at the household level. Therefore, the life cycle hypothesis has limitations when describing and explaining why consumers purchase life insurance. Black and Skipper indicated this feature of theories as normative rationales of the demand for life insurance. The name "demand for life insurance" used in the context of these two theories does not actually denote the determinant factors associated with consumer decisions to purchase life insurance; instead, it means how the purchasing quantity of life insurance shows an association with life cycle features like labor income, wealth, and bequests for beneficiaries. These two theories are generally used not to explore behavioral factors but to explore the economic demand function.

Human capital theory is based on a traditional economic perspective. Normally, in traditional economics the quality of work defined as productivity is constant among all workers. However, Schultz (1961) raised a question about the constant quality of work. Schultz suggested education and training could be an investment in workers. He stated that educated and trained workers could and should produce more than others. Schultz insisted the quality of work could be different by the degree of education and training; therefore, total productivity could be different by education and training. The education and training of workers could be a potential capital gain initially defined as human capital.

Becker (1962) explained the concept of human capital through economic functions. By developing economic functions, Becker proved that a trained worker can earn additional wages by obtaining additional education or training. In other words, if there is education or training for a worker, the effects of education or training will return as more productivity and total wage. Therefore, an investment in education or training is not only a method to improve productivity for a company but also a method to increase total wages for an individual.

There are two major features of human capital. First, human capital does not have a prompt effect on productivity and total wage; it has a potential effect. As a potential resource, human capital shifts to financial wealth during an individual's lifespan. Therefore, during the initial working period, individuals will have high human capital but low financial wealth. On the other hand, during the final working period, an individual will have low human capital but high financial wealth. Chen, Ibbotson, Milevsky, and Zhu (2006) defined consumer wealth as consisting of financial wealth and human capital. Consumer wealth is an imaginary total wealth that a person is able to expect to earn during their entire lifespan. Human capital is proxied by the potential earnings derived from the level of education or training. Financial wealth is the monetary wealth a person actually has acquired. By aging, a person receives more financial wealth, but loses human capital. In short, human capital transfers the potentiality to actual monetary wealth through aging.

The second feature of human capital comes from the first feature. Since human capital has a potential effect on productivity and total wage, there could be a risk that human capital could fail to shift toward financial wealth. Human capital has a feature of volatility. Yaari (1965) raised a major question on this risky situation and called it lifetime uncertainty. Lifetime uncertainty means an unexpected event, like a car accident, with the main wage earner in the household. Specifically, if the unexpected event is the premature death of the main wage earner, this is called mortality uncertainty. Human capital always contains uncertainty regarding the shift to financial wealth during a lifetime.

Adopting these two features of human capital on financial planning, Merton (2003) suggested the concept of lifetime consumption. For the portfolio of an individual, consumers must consider lifetime earnings and consumption. This point is linked with the previous two frameworks—the life cycle model and permanent income hypothesis. Specifically, life insurance is a hedge for the mortality risk over a person's lifespan. There could be uncertainty about an unexpected event, like premature death, during a person's lifespan. This unexpected event could be a critical threat to the financial well-being of the household. Therefore, of all the types of financial services and products needed to protect human capital or financial wealth, life insurance is of primary importance.

Theoretically, lifespan-related theories, including the life cycle model and human capital theory, explain well the reasons people need to purchase life insurance. In addition, these theories are well-supported by economic functions. However, there is a practical gap between ideal rationales and actual behavior in terms of predicting the purchase of life insurance (Black & Skipper, 2000). The concept of human life value during a lifespan suggests a reasonable rationale for purchasing life insurance. However, this is a normative reason for purchasing life insurance, which does not always relate to actual purchasing behaviors. Some consumers consider the human life value during their lifespan, but others do not consider it at all. As a result, the normative economic explanation, based on human life values during the lifespan, is a weak model to use when describing actual purchasing behaviors in the real market.

### *3.1.6 Understanding Life Insurance Demand: The Behavioral Economics Perspective*

As previously explained, lifespan-related economics does not adequately explain the reasons people purchase life insurance. These theories explain only why life insurance is needed and how the market works. To answer the question of why people purchase life insurance, there is another economic movement called behavioral economics that can be used to understand consumers' actual financial behaviors. This approach does not focus on purchasing life insurance, but focuses on general financial behavior, including insurance demand. The representative theory of behavioral economics is prospect theory.

Prospect theory comes from an economic approach blended with a psychological perspective. Kahneman and Tversky (1979) suggested researchers in economics should consider psychological factors in behavioral research. They raised a question about the basic assumptions of traditional economics. The main assumptions within traditional economics are (a) consumers pursue maximum utility and they can make decisions rationally, (b) consumers have apparent preferences, and (c) consumers have financial constraints. Specifically, of these three major assumptions within traditional economic theory assumptions, Kahneman and Tversky asked whether consumers really can engage in rational decision-making. They insisted the decision-making of consumers is possibly affected by psychological factors. Therefore, they merged psychological factors into economic functions.

Tversky and Kahneman (1992) suggested three major effects of prospect theory: (a) certainty effect, (b) reflection effect, and (c) isolation effect. First, the certainty effect denotes that consumers overweight lower probability events and underweight higher probability outcomes. In traditional economics, probability is only a linear line. However, Tversky and Kahneman suggested consumers conceptualize the probability line differently in the state of decision-making. For example, it is possible to explain why people buy a lottery ticket. Consumers overweigh the small probability of winning a lottery, so they do not care about losing money when buying lottery tickets. This is the certainty effect. Second, the reflection effect means consumers prefer to be risk averse in the case of expecting a gain. On the contrary, consumers prefer to be risk seeking when they expect to lose. In other words, consumers consider the pain from a loss to be much larger than the value from a similar gain. Third, the isolation effect explains that consumers cannot easily recognize sequential probabilities. If a consumer is exposed to a sequential situation, and the sequential situation has a different probability of occurring, then the consumer may not be able to recognize the total sum of sequential probability. Consumers generally recognize only the face probability, not the total sum of sequential probabilities.

Prospect theory implies that consumers do not always exhibit rational decision-making. Consumers are affected by psychological factors in their pursuit of maximum utility. Therefore, in terms of purchasing life insurance, prospect theory implies consumers will not always exhibit a tendency to purchase a rationally appropriate amount of life insurance. There is a limitation associated with prospect theory. Prospect theory describes only the phenomena of how people engage in seemingly irrational financial behaviors. It is hard to find influential factors on the demand for life insurance because prospect theory still leans on economic functions.

However, behavioral economics, including prospect theory, opens the possibility to consider diverse factors associated with the purchase of life insurance. In general terms of behavioral economics, psychological factors work to influence people's decision-making, regardless if it is rational or not. This happens in financial investments and risk management as well. Bodie et al. (2010) described several factors of irrational decision-making: forecasting errors, overconfidence, conservatism, representativeness bias, framing, and regret avoidance. Same as purchasing life insurance, diverse psychological factors could influence rational life insurance decision-making. As a result, prospect theory and behavioral economics, while useful, are less effective theoretical frameworks to determine which people tend to purchase life insurance and the factors that influence purchasing life insurance. However, prospect theory and behavioral economics can be used to suggest possible influential factors that interdependently interact during a person's purchase of life insurance.

### *3.1.7 Summary*

This discussion has reviewed the historical explorations of risk and risk management, actuarial science, and lifespan-related theories that are often used to support the understanding of life insurance products and the demand for life insurance. There are many possible risks faced by a household. A household needs to manage possible risks. Specifically, a risk can create a critical financial impact on a household when the risk is associated with a breadwinner's mortality. A specialized strategy to manage the mortality risk of a breadwinner is to purchase life insurance. In order to understand life insurance, diverse theories have traditionally been used to understand consumer preferences. Actuarial science supports how insurers set the price of insurance, which is the so-called equitable premium. Lifespan-related theories explain the optimal equilibrium in the life insurance market. However, as explained in Chapter 1, these two theoretical explanations are less efficient when explaining (a) which factors influence the demand for insurance and (b) how factors influence the demand for life insurance. Based on the historical contexts, this study offers an alternative theoretical framework and suggests the dynamic nonlinear systemic framework as an efficient alternative.

## References

Ando, A., & Modigliani, F. (1963). The 'life cycle' hypothesis of savings: Aggregate implications and tests. *American Economic Review, 53*(1), 55.

Becker, G. S. (1962). Investment in human capital: A theoretical analysis. *Journal of Political Economy, 70*, 9–49. https://doi.org/10.1086/258724.

Black, K., & Skipper, H. D. (2000). *Life & health insurance* (13th ed.). Upper Saddle River, NJ: Prentice Hall.

Bodie, Z., Kane, A., & Marcus, A. J. (2010). *Essentials of investments* (8th ed.). New York, NY: McGraw-Hill Irwin.

Chen, P., Ibbotson, R. G., Milevsky, M. A., & Zhu, K. X. (2006). Human capital, asset allocation, and life insurance. *Financial Analysts Journal, 62*(1), 97–109.

Clark, B. Z. (2010). Spousal life time access trusts: Planning opportunities using second-to-die life insurance policies. *Journal of Financial Services Professionals, 64*(6), 50–56.

Cordell, D. M., & Landgon, T. P. (2013). Using life insurance to fund special needs trusts. *Journal of Financial Planning, 26*(9), 34–35.

Cymbal, K. M. (2013). Choosing a family member as trustee of an irrevocable life insurance trust. *Journal of Financial Services Professionals, 67*(5), 41–52.

Dickson, D. C. M., Hardy, M., & Waters, H. R. (2013). *Actuarial mathematics for life contingent risks* (2nd ed.). Cambridge, UK: Cambridge University Press.

Fischer, S. (1973). A life cycle model of life insurance purchases. *International Economic Review, 14*, 132–152. https://doi.org/10.2307/2526049.

Kahneman, D., & Tversky, A. (1979). Prospect theory: An analysis of decision under risk. *Econometrica, 47*, 263–291. https://doi.org/10.2307/1914185.

Kait, R. E. (2012). One life insurance size doesn't fit all estate planning situations. *Journal of Financial Planning, 26*(7), 38–39.

Kling, B. (1993). *Life insurance, a non-life approach.* Amsterdam, The Nederland: Thesis Publishers.

Lewis, F. D. (1989). Dependents and the demand for life insurance. *American Economic Review, 79*(3), 452–467.

McGill, D. M., Brown, K. N., Haley, J. J., & Schieber, S. J. (2005). *Fundamentals of private pensions.* New York, NY: Oxford University Press.

Merton, R. C. (2003). Thoughts on the future: Theory and practice in investment management. *Financial Analysis Journal, 59*, 17–23. https://doi.org/10.2469/faj.v59.n1.2499.

Pissarides, C. A. (1980). The wealth-age relation with life insurance. *Economica, 47*, 451–457. https://doi.org/10.2307/2553390.

Pitacco, E., Denuit, M., Haberman, S., & Olivieri, A. (2009). *Modelling longevity dynamics for pensions and annuity business.* New York, NY: Oxford University Press.

Rejda, G. E. (2008). *Principles of risk management and insurance* (10th ed.). Boston, MA: Pearson and Addison Wesley.

Schultz, T. W. (1961). Investment in human capital. *The American Economic Review, 51*(1), 1–17.

Tannahill, B. A. (2012). Life insurance's role in retirement planning. *Journal of Financial Services Professionals, 66*(1), 33–35.

Thoyts, R. (2010). *Insurance theory and practice.* New York, NY: Routledge.

Tversky, A., & Kahneman, D. (1992). Advances in prospect theory: Cumulative representation of uncertainty. *Journal of Risk and Uncertainty, 5*, 297–323. https://doi.org/10.1007/BF00122574.

Vylder, F. D. (1997). *Life insurance theory: Actuarial perspectives*. Boston, MA: Kluwer Academic.

Whitelaw, E. R. (2014). How to relieve the plight of unskilled irrevocable life insurance trust trustees unfamiliar with their duties. *Journal of Financial Service Professionals, 68*(2), 44–49.

Yaari, M. E. (1965). Uncertain time, life insurance, and the theory of the consumer. *Review of Economic Studies, 32*, 137–150. https://doi.org/10.2307/2296058.

CHAPTER 4

# Practical Approach: Practical Approach to Personal Needs of Life Insurance with Dynamic Systemic Framework

**Abstract** Practical diversity among behavioral factors related to the demand for life insurance is explained by using this new framework (i.e., the Dynamic Systemic Framework).

**Keywords** Household-level system · Microenvironmental system · Macroenvironmental system

## 4.1 Review of Studies and Scholarly Works Related to the Research Proposed for the Analysis

As discussed in Chapter 2, the conceptual framework—the dynamic nonlinear systemic approach—is based upon two assumptions: (a) diverse systems (i.e., household level, microenvironmental, and macroenvironmental) that include many influential factors associated with the demand for life insurance and (b) many possible factors from these diverse systems are interdependently correlated with each other as a mechanism to influence the demand for life insurance. Based upon the dynamic nonlinear systemic assumptions, the following literature review provides a summary of the possible factors that could influence life insurance demand. Specifically, the conceptual framework for this study is based upon the systemic approach from Deacon and Firebaugh's (1988) ecological framework. Therefore, the conceptual taxonomy for categorizing systems follows Deacon and Firebaugh's broad concept of ecological systems:

© The Author(s) 2020
W. Heo, *The Demand for Life Insurance*,
https://doi.org/10.1007/978-3-030-36903-3_4

(a) household level, (b) microenvironmental, and (c) macroenvironmental. Looking over the diverse literature about the demand for life insurance, this review gathers relevant variables that are expected to exist in each system.

### 4.1.1 *Factors Inside the Household-Level System*

The first-order system, where this study begins, is the household-level system, which includes individual characteristics. According to Deacon and Firebaugh (1988), the household-level system includes two categories of factors—individual characteristics and family characteristics. Individual characteristic factors denote the characteristics of household members (e.g., education, training, job status, and health level). Family characteristic factors are the features of a specific family (e.g., family structure, marital status, and cultural background). According to Deacon and Firebaugh (1988), individual characteristics are categorized into three types: (a) human capital factors, (b) physical indicator factors, and (c) psychological factors.

Human capital factors include education and training, which are expected to influence life insurance demand. The initial purpose of purchasing life insurance is as a precaution for the breadwinner's death (Rejda, 2008; Thoyts, 2010) because the breadwinner is assumed to be the major income source in a household. Therefore, demand for life insurance is directly linked with the financial value that a breadwinner is able to earn for a household (Rejda). Black and Skipper (2000) defined financial value as "a measure of the actual future earnings of values of services of an individual" (p. 16). This definition is conceptually close to the concept of human capital. In other words, life insurance is a method to substitute human capital when a household faces the premature death of the breadwinner (Black & Skipper). In addition, from the perspective of the insurance industry, life insurance premiums and benefits are calculated by using estimates of human capital (Vylder, 1997). As a result, human capital is a critical factor needed to estimate life insurance demand.

Human capital is earned through education and job training. Theoretically, a person is able to earn more labor income, potentially as much as the value of one's education and job training (Becker, 1962; Schultz, 1961). Empirically, life insurance is considered to be associated with human capital, measured by education and job training (Fischer,

1973; Lewis, 1989; Li, Moshirian, Nguyen, & Wee, 2007; Lu & Yanagihara, 2013; Yaari, 1965). Specifically, using the life cycle hypothesis, Fischer (1973) and Lewis (1989) showed that education and job training are associated with the demand for life insurance. Yaari utilized the economic demand function for life insurance. He found education and the demand for life insurance have a positive association. Li et al. investigated OECD countries' life insurance markets and found the education level for each country was potentially associated with the demand for life insurance. Lu and Yanagihara discovered a recursive association between education and the demand for life insurance. Having life insurance, a household was able to secure financial resources for continuing his/her offsprings' education at the point of premature death of the breadwinner. This implies education and the purchase of life insurance are likely associated.

In summary, the representative variables for human capital—education and training—are possible influential factors when estimating the demand for life insurance. Therefore, this study uses education and job training variables as indicator variables for a breadwinner's human capital.

Physical indicator factors are thought to be associated with the demand for life insurance. Since life insurance is a precaution for the premature death of a breadwinner (Rejda, 2008; Thoyts, 2010), the breadwinner's health is a key variable a household should consider when purchasing life insurance. After reviewing the literature, no research findings were discovered to indicate physical indicator factors are directly associated with life insurance demand. However, diverse literature shows a possible indirect association between physical indicators and the demand for life insurance. Specifically, life expectancy and mortality rates significantly influence the demand for life insurance (Black & Skipper, 2000; Li et al., 2007; Thoyts, 2010). Black and Skipper (2000) introduced life expectancy as a critical environmental factor associated with the demand for life insurance. Li et al. investigated OECD countries' life insurance markets and determined life expectancy was associated with the demand for life insurance. Thoyts explained that many life insurers consider mortality rates as a major factor when finding consumers' purchasing patterns. The association between demand for life insurance and life expectancy (or mortality rate) implies the breadwinner's health issue is possibly associated with the purchase of life insurance. Therefore, this study uses several mortality-associated physical indicators that possibly influence the demand of life insurance: (a) interest in health (e.g., concern about health issues); (b) activities for health (e.g., regular moderate practice for health); and (c) harmful activities (e.g., drinking and smoking habits).

Purchasing behavior is not always rational because behavior can be prejudiced by psychological or emotional factors (Bodie, Kane, & Marcus, 2010; Kahneman & Tversky, 1979). Therefore, purchasing life insurance can be impacted by psychological factors that include emotional symptoms, risk aversion, and self-esteem. First, consumers may be influenced by bad experiences in the past (i.e., regrets) and emotional factors (i.e., depression). Bodie et al. described irrational factors on decision-making that include representativeness bias, framing, and regret avoidance. Also, in the process of financial planning, one of the major roles for purchasing life insurance is to reduce psychological uncertainty, such as anxiety (Black & Skipper, 2000). Second, Berkovitch and Venezia (1992) found the demand for life insurance is associated with risk aversion, since consumers want to receive a guarantee of financial security in the case of an unexpected premature death. This is one strategy for risk management (Thoyts, 2010). Finally, using planned behavior theory, Croy, Gerrans, and Speelman (2010) found that perceived behavioral control showed a powerful association with behavioral intention for retirement savings. Their findings imply that controllability of one's situation is associated with financial planning behavior, such as purchasing life insurance. In summary, this study employs psychological factors, including emotional factors (e.g., regret, sadness, depression, risk tolerance, and self-esteem) as possible influential factors for life insurance demand.

Family characteristics can be feasibly categorized into three factor types: (a) family structure, (b) family resource, and (c) demographic. Family structure factors include the number of family members and number of children in the household and marital status. These factors are expected to impact life insurance demand. Rejda (2008) noted that family structure and number of children are essential factors associated with the decision to purchase life insurance, which has been supported by other researchers' findings (Black & Skipper, 2000; Browne & Kim, 1993; Burnett & Palmer, 1984; Lewis, 1989; Li et al., 2007). Specifically, the number of children can be related to bequest motives, which leads to life insurance demand. In addition, a household with a higher possibility of losing a family member would likely purchase life insurance more than those with a lower possibility (Bernheim, Forni, Gokhale, & Kotlikoff, 2003; Lin & Grace, 2007). Previous findings suggest that a spouse who earns extra income can be an important factor that influences the demand for life insurance. Therefore, this study uses family structure and marital status variables as possible variables leading to life insurance demand.

Family resources are natural factors associated with life insurance demand. These possible factors include income level, wealth level, savings amount, and debt status. Fischer (1973) found financial sources for living were related to the purchase of life insurance. According to Fischer, households living on labor income purchase more life insurance, but households living off the proceeds of wealth do not purchase as much life insurance. From a macroeconomic perspective, Li et al. (2007) investigated OECD countries' life insurance markets and found income levels and social security expenditures for a country were positively associated with the demand for life insurance. In addition, Rejda (2008) introduced the following various family resource factors as being possibly associated with life insurance demand: (a) financial need at the point of the breadwinner's death (e.g., burial expenses, uninsured medical bills, installment debts, estate, inheritance, and income taxes); (b) income changes and job status changes after the breadwinner's death; (c) non-labor income sources like social security and governmental assistance; (d) specialized types of needs like mortgage redemption fund, educational needs, and emergency funds; and (e) retirement needs. Furthermore, Rejda showed that diverse types of assets can be considered factors related to purchasing life insurance, such as a house, properties, automobiles, securities and investments, checking and savings accounts, federal Social Security benefits, and other assets. Furthermore, existence of health insurance for family members is conceivably associated with the demand for life insurance. As explained by Rejda, life and health insurance are risk management strategies as a precaution of an unexpected event. Therefore, there is a feasible association between the existence of health insurance and life insurance demand. Variables of interest in this study include: income, assets, debt status, credit card usage, existence of health insurance, and governmental income assistance.

In this study, demographic factors are described by living location, urbanization, gender, and ethnic background. Black and Skipper (2000) indicated socio-demographic features (e.g., gender and ethnic background) may be associated with the demand for life insurance. Major indicators of demographic environments are household region and urbanization. For instance, industrialized areas and urbanized locations increase the demand for life insurance. Industrial systems and urbanized systems allow people to work only until a specific time, such as retirement. Black and Skipper indicated that households in diverse locations may show different demand for life insurance.

### *4.1.2 Factors from the Microenvironmental System*

Based upon the Deacon and Firebaugh (1988) taxonomy, the microenvironmental system includes (a) physical habitat (e.g., housing status and job-associated environments) and (b) social aspects (e.g., religious activities and community involvement). Housing status factors are associated with physical habitats (e.g., type of residence and mobility). Deacon and Firebaugh elucidated that space is one of the principal frameworks where households are able to manage their financial resources. Specifically, within an adequate space (e.g., financially stable household with a manageable mortgage), households can control other managerial activities, such as working, saving, and charitable giving. Besides housing status, another group of physical habitats are job-associated factors (e.g., job stability, tenure, class of worker, and spouse working status). The amount of life insurance demanded can be substituted for a breadwinner's future earnings (Black & Skipper, 2000; Rejda, 2008) associated with the breadwinner's job. Therefore, job-associated factors are thought to be associated with life insurance demand. As a result, in this study, housing status, including type of residence and mobility, and job-associated factors comprising job stability, tenure, class of worker, and spouse working status, are considered to be important variables associated with life insurance demand.

In addition to physical habitat, there are social aspects in a microenvironmental system (e.g., religious activities and community involvement) that ought to be considered. There are possible persuasive factors for life insurance demand—religious activities and community involvement. Black and Skipper (2000) explained that individuals' social surroundings could influence the demand for life insurance. Supportive social surroundings are needed for life insurance demand. As a result, mortality rate, religious activities, and community involvement are all possible indirect effective factors associated with life insurance demand.

### *4.1.3 Factors from the Macroenvironmental System*

Finally, Deacon and Firebaugh's (1988) taxonomy suggests the macroenvironmental system is essentially a societal system. This system includes (a) sociocultural, (b) political, and (c) macroeconomic factors. Sociocultural factors are broad social and cultural environments of a household (e.g., religion of community and social norms). Black and Skipper (2000) explained that an individual's broad surroundings could influence their demand for life insurance. Individuals' specific culture and religious surroundings could also affect the demand for life insurance. For instance, in Muslim religious cultures, households tend not to purchase life insurance because their religious community, as a support system, could be considered a substitute for life insurance. Social norms conceivably work as impelling factors for life insurance demand. Since social norms are not feasibly measured by individual survey questions, a proxy variable (i.e., family attitude) can be used to evaluate social norms. As such, religion of the community and social norms are used as possible influencing factors in this study.

According to Deacon and Firebaugh (1988), political factors are strongly interdependently correlated with other possible influential factors (i.e., factors from household-level system, factors from the microenvironmental system, and other factors from the macroenvironmental system). The representative variable for political factors is the political trend in an area (e.g., change of the majority party in a state and change of the governor's party in a state). Black and Skipper (2000) indicated that such political environments could be influential when estimating the demand for life insurance. For instance, political decisions about redistribution by social welfare (i.e., governmental assistance) could influence the demand for life insurance by affecting the market. In addition to the change of political trends, proxy variables can be used to evaluate social and political enforcement in an area. A possible proxy variable is the social welfare rate (i.e., governmental assistance rate) in an area.

The final group of variables includes macroeconomic factors (e.g., inflation rate and unemployment rate). Thoyts (2010) explained that many life insurers consider investment returns, inflation, interest rates, and mortality rates as major factors when estimating proper premiums. The inflation rate and interest rate lead supply; then, the supply affects the demand. Bikker, Steenbeek, and Torracchi (2012) and Love and Miller (2013) described the macroeconomic environment as an important factor linking low interest rates during long periods with demand for life insurance products. Mostly, the income level for a country is thought to be positively associated with the demand for life insurance (Gandolfi & Miners, 1996; Lewis, 1989; Truett & Truett, 1990). In terms of inflation and interest rates, high inflation or high interest rates drive consumers to seek short-term investments with high rates of return. During low inflation and interest rate environments, consumers seek long-term, safe investments. Generally, life insurance is considered a long-term investment. Therefore, inflation and interest rates generally and empirically should show a negative association with the demand for life insurance (Babbel, 1985; Outreville, 1996). As a result, macroeconomic factors should be used when estimating the demand for life insurance.

## 4.2 Summary and Analysis of the Literature as Applied to the Research Problem

The advantages associated with using a dynamic nonlinear systemic framework is the ability to use multiple layers of variables when predicting an outcome. Based on the framework, this study classifies systems into three groups: (a) household-level system, (b) microenvironmental system, and (c) macroenvironmental system. The taxonomy criteria of classifying systems and sub-characteristics of each system follow Deacon and Firebaugh's (1988) taxonomy of ecological systems.

Looking over the diverse literature about the demand for life insurance, this study utilizes numerous variables that are expected to have an association with the demand for life insurance. Reviewing the diverse literature, each possible variable is linked to each appropriate system, as shown in Table 4.1. Using the variable list in Table 4.1, this study employed ANN as the main analytic method. In other words, variables in Table 4.1 were placed into the ANN model when constructing and predicting the demand for life insurance.

**Table 4.1** Taxonomy of systems and variables in each system

| *System level* | *Characteristics of system* | *Variables* |
|---|---|---|
| Household level | Individual characteristics | Human capital: education and training |
| | | Physical indicators: interest in health, activities for health, and activity against health (alcohol drinking) |
| | | Psychological features: regrets (bad experiences in the past), emotional problem (sadness and depression), risk aversion, and self-esteem |
| | Family characteristics | Family structure: number of family members, number of children, marital status, and marital history (stability) |
| | | Family resource: income (wage), monetary assets, debt status, debt in credit card, health insurance, and governmental assistance as income |
| | | Demographics: ethnic background, region, gender, and urbanization |
| Out of household microenvironmental | Physical habitat | Job-related features: job stability (number of different jobs in the past), tenure, class of worker, spouse working status |
| | | Housing features: type of residence and mobility |
| | Social aspects | Community involvement and religious activities |
| Out of household macroenvironmental | Sociocultural environments | Cultural norm (family attitude) and belonging to religion community |
| | Political environments | Political trend and social welfare rate of an area |
| | Economic environments | Inflation rate (hardness from cost of living) and unemployment rate (number of unemployment weeks) |

## References


Babbel, D. F. (1985). The price elasticity of demand for whole life insurance. *Journal of Finance, 40*(1), 225–239. https://doi.org/10.1111/j.1540-6261.1985.tb04946.x.

Becker, G. S. (1962). Investment in human capital: A theoretical analysis. *Journal of Political Economy, 70*, 9–49. https://doi.org/10.1086/258724.

Berkovitch, E., & Venezia, I. (1992). Term vs. whole life insurance—A note. *Journal of Accounting, Auditing & Finance, 7*(2), 214–249.

Bernheim, B. D., Forni, L., Gokhale, J., & Kotlikoff, L. J. (2003). The mismatch between Life Insurance holdings and financial vulnerabilities: Evidence from the Health and Retirement Study. *The American Economic Review, 93*, 354–365. https://doi.org/10.1257/000282803321455340.

Bikker, J., Steenbeek, O. W., & Torracchi, F. (2012). The impact of scale, complexity, and service quality on the administrative costs of pension funds: A cross-country comparison. *Journal of Risk and Insurance, 79*(2), 477–514.

Black, K., & Skipper, H. D. (2000). *Life & health insurance* (13th ed.). Upper Saddle River, NJ: Prentice Hall.

Bodie, Z., Kane, A., & Marcus, A. J. (2010). *Essentials of investments* (8th ed.). New York, NY: McGraw-Hill Irwin.

Browne, M. J., & Kim, K. (1993). An international analysis of life insurance demand. *Journal of Risk & Insurance, 60*, 616–634. https://doi.org/10.2307/253382.

Burnett, J. J., & Palmer, B. A. (1984). Examining life insurance ownership through demographic and psychographic characteristics. *Journal of Risk & Insurance, 51*, 453–467. https://doi.org/10.2307/252479.

Croy, G., Gerrans, P., & Speelman, C. (2010). The role and relevance of domain knowledge, perception of planning importance, and risk tolerance in predicting savings intensions. *Journal of Economic Psychology, 31*, 860–871. https://doi.org/10.1016/j.joep.2010.06.002.

Deacon, R. E., & Firebaugh, F. M. (1988). *Family resource management: Principles and applications* (2nd ed.). Boston, MA: Allyn & Bacon.

Fischer, S. (1973). A life cycle model of life insurance purchases. *International Economic Review, 14*, 132–152. https://doi.org/10.2307/2526049.

Gandolfi, A. S., & Miners, L. (1996). Gender-based differences in life insurance ownership. *The Journal of Risk and Insurance, 63*(4), 683–693.

Kahneman, D., & Tversky, A. (1979). Prospect theory: An analysis of decision under risk. *Econometrica, 47*, 263–291. https://doi.org/10.2307/1914185.

Lewis, F. D. (1989). Dependents and the demand for life insurance. *American Economic Review, 79*(3), 452–467.

Li, D., Moshirian, F., Nguyen, P., & Wee, T. (2007). The demand for life insurance in OECD countries. *The Journal of Risk and Insurance, 74*, 637–652. https://doi.org/10.1111/j.1539-6975.2007.00228.x.

Lin, Y., & Grace, M. F. (2007). Household life cycle protection: life insurance holdings, financial vulnerability, and portfolio implications. *Journal of Risk & Insurance, 74*, 141–173. https://doi.org/10.1111/j.1539-6975.2007.00205.x.

Love, T., & Miller, W. C. (2013). Repercussions of a sustained low-interest-rate environment on life insurance products. *Journal of Financial Service Professionals, 67*(2), 44–52.

Lu, C., & Yanagihara, M. (2013). Life insurance, human capital accumulation and economic growth. *Australian Economic Papers, 52*, 52–60. https://doi.org/10.1111/1467-8454.12007.

Outreville, J. F. (1996). Life insurance markets in developing countries. *The Journal of Risk and Insurance, 63*, 263–278. https://doi.org/10.2307/253745.

Rejda, G. E. (2008). *Principles of risk management and insurance* (10th ed.). Boston, MA: Pearson Addison-Wesley.

Schultz, T. W. (1961). Investment in human capital. *The American Economic Review, 51*(1), 1–17.

Thoyts, R. (2010). *Insurance theory and practice*. New York, NY: Routledge.

Truett, D. B., & Truett, L. J. (1990). The demand for life insurance in Mexico and the United States: A comparative study. *The Journal of Risk and Insurance, 57*(2), 321–328. https://doi.org/10.2307/253306.

Vylder, F. (1997). *Life insurance theory: Actuarial perspectives*. Boston, MA: Kluwer Academic Publishers.

Yaari, M. E. (1965). Uncertain time, life insurance, and the theory of the consumer. *Review of Economic Studies, 32*, 137–150. https://doi.org/10.2307/2296058.

CHAPTER 5

# Empirical Analysis Part 1 Methodology and Data: Empirical Example of Predicting the Demand for Life Insurance by Using the Dynamic Systemic Framework

**Abstract** Herein, an empirical example of this new research will be shown. Two machine learning techniques are used for this example during unsupervised learning with clustering and supervised learning with artificial neural networks (ANNs). A basic example has been produced and confirmed using a reliable dataset from Bureau of Labor Statistics. In part 1, the research methodology and data are described.

**Keywords** National Longitudinal Survey of Youth 1979 · Individual characteristics · Family characteristics · Microenvironmental factors · Macroenvironmental factors

## 5.1 Brief Overview

This study explains why people need to manage risk and how life insurance can be an important tool for households when managing risk. Risks are uncertainties that result in chances of loss. The critical point of risks is the fact events tend to occur stochastically. In short, uncertain loss is difficult to forecast reliably. Therefore, households need to have strategies in place as a precaution for unexpected events (e.g., auto accident, house fire, premature death of household breadwinner, etc.). Purchasing insurance is one primary strategy used to transfer risk from a household to an insurer. Specifically, life insurance is a tool to transfer economic risk resulting from the premature death of a breadwinner to a life insurer.

© The Author(s) 2020

W. Heo, *The Demand for Life Insurance*,
https://doi.org/10.1007/978-3-030-36903-3_5

Reallocating risks allows households to create a relatively stable level of economic resilience after losing economic income. In addition, some life insurance products have advantages (e.g., tax savings and bequests to offspring) not offered by other products. As a result, having appropriate life insurance in a household is strongly associated with a household's well-being.

Based on a fundamental understanding of risks and life insurance, this research addresses the following questions: (a) Who purchases life insurance and (b) which factors lead people to purchase life insurance. This study investigates these initial questions on life insurance by predicting the demand for life insurance. Specifically, this investigation deals with the demand perspective from the viewpoint of consumers.

As explained in Chapters 1 and 2, pre-existing theories and frameworks (i.e., actuarial science and lifespan-related economic theories) focus on finding market equilibrium from the perspective of market-side or industrial-side interests. Actuarial science and lifespan-related economic frameworks are good at explaining the price of life insurance and the quantity sold in a market. However, these theories and frameworks are not as efficient when predicting life insurance demand or when determining influential factors of life insurance demand.

Inconsistent findings on life insurance demand have been historically assumed to be caused by the existence of an interdependent correlation among numerous predictor factors. Specifically, previous theories and frameworks have most often used a linear assumption to find influential factors associated with life insurance demand. In short, nearly all pre-existing theories and frameworks focus on partial covariance (i.e., marginal effects) among specific variables selected by researchers. However, from the perspective that diverse factors are interdependently correlated with each other, partial covariance is a less efficient way to explain life insurance demand. A more robust approach is one based on a theoretical framework that assumes the existence of interdependent correlations among possible influential factors on life insurance demand, namely the ecologically systemic perspective and nonlinear science.

An ecological system, which was introduced by Deacon and Firebaugh (1988), can be used as a theoretical framework for use in understanding life insurance demand. It is hypothesized in this study that many possible influential factors from various systems (e.g., household, microenvironmental, and macroenvironmental) interdependently correlate and produce a phenomenon. The interdependent correlations among many possible influential factors are feasibly seen as dynamic nonlinear associations. Therefore, nonlinear science was adopted here as a methodological background to investigate the dynamic interdependent relationships explained by the ecological system. As a result, this study adopted two major perspectives and produced a main framework—a dynamic nonlinear systemic framework.

Based on the theoretical framework from Chapter 2, the main questions for this study are: (a) Does categorizing people into sub-samples (clustering) improve the discovery of influential variables on the demand for life insurance? (b) What factors, from a consumer's perspective, are important to determine life insurance demand? And (c) does the usage of a dynamic nonlinear systemic (e.g., the artificial neural) network improve the prediction rate for the demand of life insurance compared to other econometric models (i.e., logistic estimation)? To answer these questions, the main empirical methodology utilized was an artificial neural network (ANN). In addition to the main methodology, cluster analysis was incorporated into the study to answer the first question. Finally, to compare the prediction level of methodologies, multinomial logistic regression was used.

## 5.2 Design of the Study and Methods

### *5.2.1 Description of Data*

To answer the research questions, this study used nationwide panel data from the National Longitudinal Survey of Youth (NLSY79) from 2004 to 2012. The Bureau of Labor Statistics (BLS) sponsored this survey. In 1979, the BLS recruited the first 12,686 respondents and surveyed the same sample every two years. The initial cohort survey sample was born between 1957 and 1964 (Bureau of Labor Statistics, 2014). Therefore, the initial cohort was age 14–22 in 1979. Respondents' ages were from 45 to 53 in 2010. Over 30 years, the initial survey participants declined because of eligibility issues and attrition. As a result, the sample was reduced to 7565 in 2010 (see Table 5.1). Among the 7565 samples, some respondents failed to answer the survey questions that were used in the study (e.g., education level, training, health intention, healthy activities, average drinking, sadness, depression, risk aversion, self-esteem, experience of death, tenure weeks, spouse working weeks, marital status, number of children, governmental income, monetary assets, debt status,

**Table 5.1** Sample size by year in the NLSY79 dataset

| *Year* | *Sample size* |
|---|---|
| 1979 | 12,686 |
| 1984 | 12,069 |
| 1990 | 10,436 |
| 1994 | 8891 |
| 1998 | 8399 |
| 2000 | 8033 |
| 2002 | 7724 |
| 2004 | 7661 |
| 2006 | 7654 |
| 2008 | 7757 |
| 2010 | 7565 |
| Final data | 4680 |

*Source* https://www.nlsinfo.org/content/cohorts/nlsy79/intro-to-the-sample/nlsy79-sample-introduction

credit card debt, home ownership, religious activities, family conservativeness, and economic difficulties). As a result, the final sample size for this study was 4680.

The NLSY79 is a nationwide dataset representing the US population. This means the dataset has external validity, which increases generalizability. The selected variables, as described below, were considered valid constructs for internal validity. In summary, the usage of the NLSY79 dataset ensured a representative, reliable, and valid sample. For missing data, this research study employed a list-wise deleting imputation method.

The dependent variable of this study, the ownership of cash value life insurance, was measured in two survey years (2008 and 2012). Variables from 2010 were used in the models. However, some variables in 2012 were used in the analyses since they were considered to have a cumulative feature between 2008 and 2012. Variables from the 2012 survey were total number of bad experiences, total monetary assets, total investments in bonds, and credit card debt. A few variables were measured in 2004 and 2006 that were needed in the statistical model. Family attitude was assessed in 2004 and self-esteem was surveyed in 2006. These were assumed to be consistent over several years.

In addition to survey data from the NLSY79, this study used two other measures from the National Governors Association and US Census Bureau. Specifically, in the case of macroenvironmental systems, the NLSY79 did not have enough information about respondents' party affiliations. Therefore, data from National Governors Association and

US Census Bureau were merged into NLSY79 based on respondent area codes. A detailed explanation will be presented later to introduce each variable's measurement.

### 5.2.2 *Dependent Variables from the Data*

The criterion variable for this study was change of life insurance ownership. Respondents in the 2008 survey answered a question related to having cash value life insurance and not having life insurance:

> *Do you [or] [Spouse/partner's name] have any cash-value life insurance policies?*

A similar question was asked in 2012. A change in life insurance ownership between 2008 and 2012 was coded as three categories: $-1$ = dropped life insurance ownership, $0$ = no change in life insurance ownership, and $1$ = purchased life insurance.

### 5.2.3 *Independent Variables from the Data*

Based on the literature review, the following possible influential factors thought to be associated with the demand for life insurance were selected: human capital factors, physical status, psychological factors, family structure, family resources, demographics, job-related factors, housing features, community involvement, cultural norms, political trends, and economic situations. Based on the main framework of this study—dynamic nonlinear systemic framework—selected factors were categorized into three systems: (a) household level, (b) microenvironmental, and (c) macroenvironmental.

#### 5.2.3.1 *Individual Characteristics Individual Characteristics in the Household-Level System*

There are two major sub-categories in the household-level system: individual characteristics and family characteristics. The sub-category of individual characteristics has three major factors, as suggested in the literature describing individual characteristics: (a) human capital factors, (b) physical status factors, and (c) psychological factors. Variables for these individual characteristics were measured with NLSY79 survey questions (see Table 5.2).

As shown in Table 5.2, individual characteristic variables in the household-level system were matched with selected factors from the literature. First, human capital factors included measures for education level and existence of training. Education level was measured in 2010 as an ordinal variable: 1 = high school graduate, 2 = college level degree, and 3 = over graduate degree. Besides education level, the existence of any training, including on-the-job training, was assessed to measure human capital as a binary variable: 1 = having a vocational training/job training and 0 = not having a vocational training/job training.

Second, physical status factors were measured using three variables: (a) interest in health, (b) activity for better health, and (c) activity against better health. Interest in health was measured by asking if a respondent was concerned about food information. The following two questions

**Table 5.2** Individual characteristic variables from NLSY79 matched with selected factors

| *Factors from literature* | *Variables from NLSY79* | | |
|---|---|---|---|
| | *Measurement (survey year)* | *Variable type* | *Code* |
| Human capital factors | Education level (2010) | Ordinal | Less than or equal to high school graduate = 1<br>College level degree = 2<br>Over graduate degree = 3 |
| | Existence of training (2010) | Binary | Yes = 1<br>No = 0 |
| Physical status factors | Interest in health (2010) | Scale | Always = 5<br>Often = 4<br>Sometimes = 3<br>Rarely = 2<br>Never = 1 |
| | Activity for better health (2010) | Numeric | Total number of health activities per week |
| | Activity against better health (2010) | Numeric | Total number of drinking cans/glasses of alcohol |
| Psychological features | Experience of family member's death (until 2012) | Numeric | Total number of death experience in family: number of miscarriages/stillbirths, number of parents death, and number of abortions |

(continued)

**Table 5.2** (continued)

| *Factors from literature* | *Variables from NLSY79* | | |
|---|---|---|---|
| | *Measurement (survey year)* | *Variable type* | *Code* |
| | Sadness (compiled over years) | Scale | Rarely/None of the time/1 Day = 0<br>Some/A little of the time/1–2 Days = 1<br>Occasionally/Moderate amount/3–4 Days = 2<br>Most/All of the time/5–7 Days = 3 |
| | Depression (compiled over years) | Scale | Rarely/None of the time/1 Day = 0<br>Some/A little of the time/1–2 Days = 1<br>Occasionally/Moderate amount/3–4 Days = 2<br>Most/All of the time/5–7 Days = 3 |
| | Risk aversion (2010) | Scale | Highly risk averse = 4<br>Medium-high risk averse = 3<br>Medium-low risk averse = 2<br>Low risk averse = 1 |
| | Self-esteem (2006) | Numeric | Total sum of 10 questions by using,<br>Strongly agree = 4<br>Agree = 3<br>Disagree = 2<br>Strongly disagree = 1 |

were asked using a 5-point scale: 5 = always, 4 = often, 3 = sometimes, 2 = rarely, and 1 = never. The mean value of two questions was used for assessing the interest in health of respondents:

*A*: When you buy a food item for the first time, how often would you say you read the nutritional information sometimes listed on the label—would you say always, often, sometimes, rarely, or never?

*B*: When you buy a food item for the first time, how often would you say you read the ingredient list on the package—would you say always, often, sometimes, rarely, or never?

Activity for better health was measured by two questions asking how many times respondents exercised weekly. The variable, activities for better health, was coded as a numeric variable summing up the total number of two activities per week:

*C*: How often do you do vigorous activities for at least 10 minutes that cause heavy sweating or large increases in breathing or heart rate?
*D*: How often do you do light or moderate activities for at least 10 minutes that cause only light sweating or slight to moderate increase in breathing or heart rate?

Activities detrimental to better health were measured by how many cans or glasses of alcohol a respondent drank the previous month:

*E*: On the days that you drink, about how many drinks do you have on the average day? By a drink, we mean the equivalent of a can of beer, a glass of wine, or a shot glass of hard liquor.

Third, psychological factors were measured with five variables: (a) proxy variable for regret (i.e., bad experience in the past); (b) emotional problems (i.e., sadness and depression); (c) variable for risk tolerance (i.e., risk aversion); (d) proxy variable for time orientation (impatience); and (e) self-esteem. The proxy variable for regret was experiencing a family members' death in the past; specifically, death experiences associated with life (i.e., number of miscarriages/stillbirths, number of parents' death, and number of abortions) were used to proxy regret. Experience of family members' death was coded as a numeric variable summing up the total number of miscarriages/stillbirths, parents' death, and total number of abortions.

Emotional problems were measured by two variables: sadness and depression. Each question shown below was asked using a 4-point scale ranging from 0 to 3:

*F*: During the past week, I felt depressed.
*G*: During the past week, I felt sad.

Respondents answered using a 4-point scale on the two questions, respectively, with 0 = rarely/none of the time/1 day, 1 = some/a little of the time/1–2 days, 2 = occasionally/moderate amount/3–4 days, and 3 = most/all of the time/5–7 days. Respondents were asked over a number of years about these two emotional states after attaining 40 years of age. Compiling answers about these questions over a number of years, two representative variables for sadness and depression were generated in the NLSY79 dataset. These two variables were used to represent respondents' emotional features regardless of specific survey years.

Risk aversion was evaluated using three sequential questions which were assessed in 2010. The first question was:

> *H*: Suppose that you are the only income earner in the family, and that you have to choose between two new jobs. The first job would guarantee your current total family income for life. The second job is possibly better paying, but the income is also less certain. There is a 50-50 chance the second job would increase your total lifetime income by 20% and a 50-50 change that it would cut it by 10%. Which job would you take: the first job or the second job?

Those who answered the "first job" were asked Question *I* below and those who answered the "second job" were asked Question *J*.

> *I*: Suppose the chances were 50-50 that the second job would increase your total lifetime income by 20%, and 50-50 that it would cut it by five percent. Would you take the first job or the second job?
>
> *J*: Suppose the chances were 50-50 that the second job would increase your total lifetime income by 20%, and 50-50 that it would cut it by 15%. Would you take the first job or the second job?

Those who answered the "first job" in Questions *H* and *I* were considered to have high risk tolerance; if the respondent answered "second job" in Question *I*, they were considered to have moderately high risk tolerance. Those who answered the "first job" in Question *J* were considered to have moderately low risk tolerance; if the respondent answered the "second job" in Question *J*, they were considered to have low risk tolerance. Risk aversion (the inverse of risk tolerance) was coded on a 4-point scale: 4 = Highly risk averse, 3 = Medium-high risk averse, 2 = Medium-low risk averse, and 1 = Low risk averse.

Self-esteem was measured using Rosenberg's self-esteem scale. The self-esteem questions were asked in 2006. It was assumed that self-esteem was a consistent personal feature. The question set consisted of ten items with a 4-point scale: 4=strongly agree, 3=agree, 2=disagree, and 1=strongly disagree. A numeric value was estimated by summing all of the following 10 questions. Calculating a total sum of the 10 items, this self-esteem item was coded as a numeric variable: maximum number=40 (i.e., high self-esteem) and minimum number=10 (i.e., low self-esteem).

*K*: Now I'm going to read a list of opinions people have about themselves. After I read each statement, please tell me how much you strongly agree, agree, disagree, or strongly disagree with these opinions.
*a.* "I feel that I'm a person of worth, at least on equal basis with others."
*b.* "I feel that I have a number of good qualities."
*c.* "All in all, I am inclined to feel that I am a failure."
*d.* "I am able to do things as well as most other people"
*e.* "I feel that I do not have much to be proud."
*f.* "I take a positive attitude toward myself."
*g.* "On the whole, I am satisfied with myself."
*h.* "I wish I could have more respect for myself."
*i.* "I certainly feel useless at times."
*j.* "At times I think I am no good at all."

#### *5.2.3.2 Family Characteristics in the Household-Level System*

Three factors emerged from the literature related to family characteristics: (a) family structure, (b) family resources, and (c) demographic factors. Variables for these family characteristics were measured with survey questions shown in Table 5.3.

Family size, marital status, marital stability, and number of children were used as family structure factors. The number of family members in 2010 determined the family size. Since life insurance is strongly associated with the existence of a spouse (i.e., survivor), marital status in 2010 was measured as a binary variable: 0=without spouse and 1=with spouse. Marital history in 2010 was measured as the number of previous spouses reported by a respondent. Since marital status is considered an influential factor on the demand for life insurance, the number of spouses in the past was thought to be possibly associated with the possession of life insurance. This variable was coded as a numeric variable: 0=never have spouse/partner, 1=current is the first spouse/partner, 2=current is the second spouse/partner, 3=current is the third

**Table 5.3** Household-level system variables from NLSY79 matched with selected factors

| *Factors from Literature* | *Variables from NLSY79* | | |
|---|---|---|---|
| | *Measurement (survey year)* | *Variable type* | *Code* |
| Family structure factors | Family size (2010) | Numeric | Number of family members |
| | Marital status (2010) | Binary | With spouse = 1<br>Without spouse = 0 |
| | Marital stability (2010) | Numeric | Never have spouse/partner = 0<br>Current is the first spouse/partner = 1<br>Current is the second spouse/partner = 2<br>Current is the third spouse/partner = 3<br>Current is the fourth spouse/partner = 4<br>Current is the fifth spouse/partner = 5<br>Current is the sixth spouse/partner = 6<br>Current is the seventh spouse/partner = 7 |
| | Number of children (2010) | Numeric | Number of children in a household |
| Family resource factors | Labor income (2010) | Numeric | Family net income (dollar) |
| | Governmental assistance (2010) | Numeric | Dollar amount to earn from governmental assistance |
| | Total money assets (2012) | Numeric | Dollar amount |
| | Total cash in bonds (2012) | Numeric | Dollar amount |
| | Debt status (2012) | Nominal | Be in debt = -1<br>Break even = 0<br>Having something left over = 1 |
| | Credit card Debt (2012) | Binary | Having debt = 1<br>Not having debt = 0 |
| | Existence of health insurance (2010) | Binary | Having health insurance = 1<br>Not having health insurance = 0 |
| Demographic features | Race | Nominal | White (Yes = 1; No = 0)<br>Hispanic (Yes = 1; No = 0)<br>Black or African-American (Yes = 1; No = 0) |

(continued)

**Table 5.3** (continued)

| *Factors from Literature* | *Variables from NLSY79* | | |
|---|---|---|---|
| | *Measurement (survey year)* | *Variable type* | *Code* |
| | | | Asian (Yes = 1; No = 0)<br>Native Hawaiian or Pacific Islander (Yes = 1; No = 0)<br>American Indian or Alaska native (Yes = 1; No = 0)<br>Some other race (Yes = 1; No = 0) |
| | Gender | Binary | Male = 1<br>Female = 0 |
| | Rural or Urban (2010) | Nominal | Not in SMSA (Yes = 1; No = 0)<br>SMSA but not central city (Yes = 1; No = 0)<br>SMSA in central city (Yes = 1; No = 0)<br>SMSA but central city not known (Yes = 1; No = 0) |
| | Region (2010) | Nominal | Northeast (Yes = 1; No = 0)<br>North central (Yes = 1; No = 0)<br>South (Yes = 1; No = 0)<br>West (Yes = 1; No = 0) |

*Note* Due to sample size restriction, the analyses were completed with White, Black, and Hispanic

spouse/partner, 4 = current is the fourth spouse/partner, 5 = current is the fifth spouse/partner, 6 = current is the sixth spouse/partner, and 7 = current is the seventh spouse/partner. The number of children in 2010 was coded as an ordinal variable.

Family resource factors are variables associated with family financial management. In the data from the NLSY79, few respondents answered questions regarding net total family income, total monetary assets, and debt status. It is generally difficult to obtain correct answers about these types of questions. Therefore, in this study, alternative variables in the NLSY79 were used to estimate family income, monetary assets, and debt status. Labor income and governmental assistance were used to estimate family income. To measure monetary assets, total money assets and total money in bonds were utilized. For assessing debts in a household, asset status and existence of credit card debt were used.

In terms of the family income variable, truncated total net family income was utilized in the analyses. To include governmental assistance as non-labor income, governmental assistance (i.e., total amount of Aid to Families with Dependent Children, food stamps, Supplemental Security Income, and other governmental welfare) in 2010 was measured as a dollar amount. In the case of monetary assets, total money assets in a household were measured as a dollar amount by combining all monetary assets (i.e., checking account, savings account, and money market account) that both a respondent and spouse reported holding in a household. Since monetary assets were able to change during the survey periods, the monetary asset variable from 2012 was used in this study as the final monetary assets of a household. In addition to total money assets, total cash amounts held in bonds from the 2012 survey was measured to complement total money assets.

Debt status was measured using the following question, which was surveyed in 2012:

> *L*: Suppose you [and] [Spouse/partner's name] were to sell all of your major possessions (including your home), turn all of your investments and other assets into cash, and pay all of your debts. Would you have something left over, break even, or be in debt?

Using this question, debt status was coded as a nominal variable: −1 = be in debt, 0 = break even, and 1 = have something left over. In addition, a second debt question was used:

> *M*: Do you [or] [Spouse/partner's name] have any credit cards or owe money on any credit card accounts, such as Visa, American Express or credit cards for specific stores, such as department stores or gas stations?

The answer for Question *M* was dichotomous (Yes/No). Therefore, it was coded as a binary variable: 1 = having a credit debt and 0 = not having a credit debt.

As explained in previous chapters, the existence of health insurance is feasibly associated with the demand for life insurance. Therefore, having health insurance in 2010 was considered a family resource factor. Existence of health insurance covering respondents, spouses, and their children was measured as a binary variable, respectively: 1 = having health insurance and 0 = not having health insurance.

Third, socio-demographic features for families were measured. Race was categorized as White, Black or African-American, Asian, native

Hawaiian or Pacific Islander, American Indian or Alaska native, some other race, and none specified. All race responses were coded as dummy variables (i.e., White = 1 and others = 0; Hispanic = 1 and other = 0; African-American = 1 and others = 0; Asian = 1 and others = 0; native Hawaiian or Pacific Islander = 1 and others = 0; American Indian or Alaska native = 1 and others = 0; and some other race = 1). Gender was coded as binary variable: 1 = male and 0 = female. Region in 2010 was divided into four areas: northeast, north central, south, and west. Northeast included the states of Connecticut, Maine, Massachusetts, New Hampshire, New Jersey, New York, Pennsylvania, Rhode Island, and Vermont. North central covered the states of Illinois, Indiana, Iowa, Kansas, Michigan, Minnesota, Missouri, Nebraska, North Dakota, Ohio, South Dakota, and Wisconsin. South area contained the states of Alabama, Arkansas, Delaware, District of Columbia, Florida, Georgia, Kentucky, Louisiana, Maryland, Mississippi, North Carolina, Oklahoma, South Carolina, Tennessee, Texas, Virginia, and West Virginia. West area comprised the states of Alaska, Arizona, California, Colorado, Hawaii, Idaho, Montana, Nevada, New Mexico, Oregon, Utah, Washington, and Wyoming. All answers to the region question were coded as dummy variables (i.e., northeast = 1 and others = 0; north central = 1 and others = 0; south = 1 and others = 0; and west = 1 and others = 0). Living area surveyed in 2010 was measured by standard metropolitan statistical area (SMSA): not in SMSA, SMSA but not central city, SMSA in central city, and SMSA but central city not known. All living area responses were coded as dummy variables (i.e., not in SMSA = 1 and others = 0; SMSA but not central city = 1 and others = 0; SMSA in central city = 1 and others = 0; and SMSA but central city not known = 1 and others = 0).

#### *5.2.3.3 Variables in the Microenvironmental System*

The microenvironmental system has two major sub-categories: physical habitat and social aspect factors. First, physical habitat factors are job-related variables and housing features. Second, social aspect factors are type of residence and mobility. Variables for the microenvironmental system are shown in Table 5.4.

Job-related variables were used from the 2010 survey. Variables included the number of different jobs ever taken (i.e., individual job stability), total tenure in weeks, class of worker, and number of spouse working weeks. Number of different jobs ever reported, as of the interview date, was measured for each individual. Total tenure in weeks was

**Table 5.4** Microenvironmental system variables from NLSY79 matched with selected factors

| *Factors from literature* | *Variables from NLSY79* | | |
|---|---|---|---|
| | *Measurement (survey year)* | *Variable type* | *Code* |
| Physical habitat factors (Jobs) | Number of jobs ever taken (2010) | Numeric | Number of different jobs that a respondent has ever taken in the past |
| | Total tenure in weeks (2010) | Numeric | Number of weeks tenured with employers up to five |
| | Class of worker (2010) | Nominal | Government worker (Yes = 1; No = 0) Private for-profit company worker (Yes = 1; No = 0) Non-profit organization worker (Yes = 1; No = 0) Self-employed (Yes = 1; No = 0) Working in family business (Yes = 1; No = 0) |
| | Number of spouse working weeks (2010) | Numeric | Number of working weeks by spouse |
| Physical habitat factors (Housing) | Mobility (2010) | Binary | Move = 1 Not move = 0 |
| | Residency (2010) | Binary | Own house = 1 Not own house = 0 |
| Social aspect factors | Religious activities (2012) | Scale | More than once a week = 6 About once a week = 5 Two or three times a month = 4 About once a month = 3 Several times or less during the year = 2 Not at all = 1 |
| | Community involvement (2006) | Binary | 1 = Participant 0 = Non-participant |

reported as the total number of weeks a respondent had tenure from all employers up to five. Class of worker was asked for the primary job. This was divided into five categories. These included government worker, private for-profit company worker, non-profit organization worker, self-employed, and working in family business. All answers in class of worker were coded as dummy variables (i.e., government worker = 1 and others = 0; private for-profit company worker = 1 and others = 0; non-profit organization worker = 1 and others = 0; self-employed = 1 and other = 0; and working in family business = 1 and others = 0). The number of a spouse working weeks was measured by the actual number of weeks worked per/year.

Housing variables were residence type and mobility surveyed in 2010. The residence type was measured as a binary variable: 1 = living in owned dwelling unit and 0 = living in non-owned dwelling unit. Mobility was measured with the following item:

> *N*: Since that time, have you moved to another state, city, or county?

Mobility was measured as a dichotomous variable and coded: 1 = moved and 0 = not moved.

Social aspect factors include religious activities, aging trend measured by mortality rate, and community involvement. Religious activities were surveyed and measured with the following question:

> *O*: In the past year, about how often have you attended religious services? More than once a week, about once a week, two or three times a month, about once a month, several times or less during the year, or not at all?

As respondents and spouses were required to answer on a 6-point scale, the question was coded as: 6 = more than once a week, 5 = about once a week, 4 = two or three times a month, 3 = about once a month, 2 = several times or less during the year, and 1 = not at all.

Community involvement was surveyed in 2006 and measured as a binary variable: 1 = participate in community activities and 0 = not participate in community activities. The original question was:

> *P*: We are interested in any volunteer work you may have performed recently. In the past 12 months did you do achieve any unpaid volunteer work?

#### *5.2.3.4 Variables in the Macroenvironmental System*

The macroenvironmental system includes three major groups of factors: sociocultural environments, political environments, and economic environments. Variables for the macroenvironmental system were measured with the survey questions shown in Table 5.5. In addition to the survey questions from the NLSY79, sources from the National Governors Association and US Census Bureau were merged into the NLSY79 dataset as a way to measure political trends in an area. Detailed information will be introduced on the measurement of the political trend variable later in this section.

**Table 5.5** Macroenvironmental system variables from NLSY79 matched with selected factors

| *Factors from literature* | *Variables from NLSY79* | | |
|---|---|---|---|
| | *Measurement* | *Variable type* | *Code* |
| Sociocultural environmental factors | Belonging to religious community (2012) | Nominal | Roman Catholic (Yes = 1; No = 0)<br>Protestant Christian (Yes = 1; No = 0)<br>Jewish (Yes = 1; No = 0)<br>Others (Yes = 1; No = 0)<br>No religion (Yes = 1; No = 0) |
| | Family attitude (2004) | Numeric | Total sum of 7 questions by using,<br>Highly conservative = 4<br>Conservative = 3<br>Liberal = 2<br>Highly liberal = 1 |
| Political environmental factors | Welfare rate (2010) | Numeric | Ratio of how many people gets governmental assistance |
| | Political trend (2010) | Numeric | Ratio of how many politicians affiliate to conservative party (Republican rate)<br>Liberal party (Democrat): reference group |
| Economic environmental factors | Number of unemployed weeks (2010) | Numeric | Number of unemployed weeks of a respondent |
| | Hardness from cost of living (2010) | Scale | Strongly agree = 4<br>Agree = 3<br>Disagree = 2<br>Strongly disagree = 1 |

Two variables were used as sociocultural environmental factors. Belonging to a religious community was assessed in 2012. Answers were divided into five categories: Roman Catholic, Protestant Christian, Jewish, others, and no religion. Since each religious community was a nominal variable, the five categories were coded as dummy variables (i.e., Roman Catholic = 1 and others = 0; Protestant Christian = 1 and others = 0; Jewish = 1 and others = 0; Other religious community = 1 and others = 0; and No religion = 1 and others = 0). To measure social norms, family attitude as of 2004 was used as a proxy variable for adopting social norms. The survey used seven items with a 4-point scale (i.e., strongly agree, agree, disagree, and strongly disagree) as shown below. Since two questions, among seven questions, were asked using a negative code, two questions including *(c)* and *(f)* were reverse coded. Calculating the total sum of seven questions, the family attitude variables were coded as a numeric variable: maximum number = 28 (i.e., highly conservative) and minimum number = 7 (i.e., highly liberal).

> *R*: We are interested in your opinion about the employment of wives. I will read a series of statements and after each one I would like to know whether you strongly agree, agree, disagree, or strongly disagree.
> *a*. "A woman's place is in the home, not in the office or shop."
> *b*. "A wife who carries out her full family responsibilities doesn't have time for outside employment."
> *c*. "A working wife feels more useful than one who doesn't hold a job."
> *d*. "The employment of wives leads to more juvenile delinquency."
> *e*. "It is much better for everyone concerned if the man is the achiever outside the home, and the woman takes care of the home and family."
> *f*. "Men should share the work around the house with women, such as doing wash dishes, cleaning, and so forth."
> *g*. "Women are much happier if they stay at home and take care of their children."

Second, political environmental factors were represented by the welfare ratio for the area and political trends. The welfare ratio for the area was measured by the ratio of how many respondents received governmental assistance (i.e., Aid to Families with Dependent Children, food stamps, Supplemental Security Income, and other governmental welfare) in each area. In the NLSY79 dataset, there were four areas (i.e., northeast, north central, south, and west) as explained previously. In one specific area, the welfare ratio was calculated by using the number of people who received governmental assistance to the total number of respondents. Specifically, the number of people who obtained governmental assistance in one area was divided by the total number of respondents in the same area. Therefore, the welfare ratio was measured as a numeric variable.

Political trend was measured by combining data from NLSY79 with data from the National Governors Association (2015) and the US Census Bureau (2015). Data from the National Governors Association contained each state's governors' political affiliation in 2010; data from US Census Bureau included representatives' and senators' political affiliations in 2010. Since the NLSY79 survey mainly focuses on individual level or household-level questions, macro-level data (i.e., politician's party in each state) were not assessed in the dataset. Substitute data issued by National Governors Association and US Census Bureau were merged into the NLSY79 dataset. Specifically, political affiliations of governors, senators, and representatives in each state in 2010 were merged into NLSY79. To measure political trends, 51 state codes in the National Governors Association and US Census Bureau data were transformed into four area codes matching with the NLSY79 (i.e., northeast, north central, south, and west). In each area, the ratio between conservative politicians and liberal politicians was used to indicate the area's political trend. Specifically, by setting Democrat politicians as the reference group, the ratio of Republican politician numbers divided by total number of politicians in each four area was used as a numeric variable.

Economic environmental factors were measured using two variables: unemployment rate and difficulties from a rise in the cost of living. The unemployment rate was measured by the number of unemployed weeks reported by each respondent, which was the number of unemployed weeks during the last one year. Difficulties from a rise in the cost of living represented subjective feelings of the inflation rate. The following question was used to assess difficulties from a rise in the cost of living using a 4-point scale: 4 = strongly agree, 3 = agree, 2 = disagree, and 1 = strongly disagree:

> *S*: We are interested in your opinion about the employment of wives. I will read a series of statements and after each one I would like to know whether you strongly agree, agree, disagree, or strongly disagree. "Employment of both parents is necessary to keep up with the high cost of living."

### 5.2.4 *Data Analysis Procedure*

To answer the research questions described in previous chapters, two major analytical phases were used in this study. In the first phase, a clustering model was used to check the improvement of discovery of influential variables among categorized sub-samples. In the second phase, prediction rates among different methodologies were evaluated.

#### *5.2.4.1 Clustering the Sub-Sample for Better Discovery of a Variable List*

As described in previous chapters, one of the main research questions of this study was: Does categorizing consumers into sub-samples improve the discovery of influential variables influencing the demand for life insurance? To answer this question, a clustering methodology was employed. Specifically, a hierarchical clustering model with Ward's linkage algorithm was used for this study. The criteria variables for clustering were selected from the socio-demographic variables (i.e., education level, marital status, family size, monetary assets, and gender). Using many criteria variables to divide sub-samples makes it difficult to specify sub-samples (Mirkin, 2011). The main algorithm of the clustering linkage was Ward's method. Ward's linkage method is sometimes called other names, like the minimum-variance method and error-sum-of-squares method. As the other names denote, Ward's linkage method minimizes the variances of selected variables (i.e., education level, family size, labor income, and gender). Ward's method is the most appropriate to use in the case of multivariable normal and spherical groups (Kaufman & Rousseeuw, 1990). Using Ward's linkage method as the hierarchical clustering model, the study was expected to have a few sub-samples. However, among the sub-samples found by clustering, a few sub-samples were not utilized in the next multinomial logistic regression and ANN analyses because of sample size restrictions. Specifically, sub-samples that had a sample size of less than 200 were excluded in the next analyses. Following the clustering analysis, this study examined the prediction rate of ANN as a way to improve the prediction rate.

#### *5.2.4.2 Prediction Rate Comparison*

In order to check the efficiency of ANN as a tool for predicting life insurance demand, a logistic model was used as a comparison methodology. Two methodologies, including ANN and multinomial logistic regression, were implemented twice. The purpose of the first implementation of methodologies was to find an optimal ANN and multinomial logistic model for predicting life insurance demand. The purpose of the second operation was to check the predicting power of the two methodologies. In short, the second operation was used to check how the optimal models found in phase one predicted life insurance demand. In order to implement each methodology twice, the total sample was divided into two groups. Using R programming, one-half of respondents were randomly selected as a training dataset. The first half was used to find an optimal model for the three methodologies. The other half, called the test data, was used to predict life insurance demand using the optimal model found using the training data.

As explained in Chapter 1, the basic functions of ANN are shown below:

$$u = \sum_{i=1}^{n} \omega_i \chi_i \tag{5.1}$$

$$y = f(u - \theta) \tag{5.2}$$

where $u$ denotes the activation unit to reach the function ($f$), $\chi_i$ are input variables and $\omega_i$ is the weight for each variable; θ is a threshold to activate the function ($f$); the output ($y$) is calculated when the activation unit ($u$) has a number over threshold ($\theta$). The basic functions assume that there is one association between the dependent variable and hidden layer ($u$). However, one hidden layer is not appropriate if there are many influential factors. Therefore, it was assumed that there are optimal numbers of hidden layers in the ANN model as shown in the function below. The function includes additional hidden layers by using additional weights ($\omega_j$).

$$y = f\left(\sum_{j=1}^{m} \omega_j \bullet f\left(\sum_{i=1}^{n} \omega_{ij} \chi_i\right)\right) \tag{5.3}$$

To find the optimal number of hidden layers, error rates by the number of hidden layers were checked. When the error rate report was at the minimum level, the number of hidden layers was selected as the optimal number. With the optimal number of hidden layers, the ideal ANN (optimal) model was selected and used on the test dataset to predict life insurance demand. The predicting power was estimated using a ratio, which was the number of correctly predicted respondents divided by the total number of respondents.

In order to check the prediction rate of the multinomial logistic model, the following statistical function was used:

$$\ln\left[\frac{\text{Prob}\,(y=i)}{\text{Prob}\,(y=j)}\right]=\sum_{k=1}^{K}\beta_{jk}X_k \tag{5.4}$$

where $X_k$ denotes all influential factors including household-level system factors, microenvironmental system factors, and macroenvironmental system factors. The reference group for the multinomial logistic regression ($y=j$) was the no change group of life insurance ownership. Using the training dataset, the relative risk ratio (RRR), which was the odds ratio ($OR$) of the multinomial logistic model, was found. Same as the previous two methodologies, the RRR from the multinomial logistic model was inspected to check how well it predicts life insurance demand.

#### 5.2.4.3 *Statistics Programs for Analyses*

Two statistics programs were used for the analysis procedure. Two statistical programs (i.e., STATA 12.0 and RStudio) were used to code, clean variables, and randomize sampling in order to divide the dataset, ANN estimation/prediction, multinomial logistic estimation/prediction, and clustering models.

## 5.3 Summary

This chapter has described the research questions of interest in this study. Additionally, the dataset was introduced. Specific variables were matched to the conceptual model. Finally, the data analysis procedures were discussed. The remainder of this dissertation presents the results from the analyses. The next chapter summarizes findings and presents an applied discussion.

## References

Bureau of Labor Statistics. (2014). *The NLSY79 sample: An introduction.* Retrieved from https://www.nlsinfo.org/content/cohorts/nlsy79/intro–to–the–sample/nlsy79–sample–introduction.

Deacon, R. E., & Firebaugh, F. M. (1988). *Family resource management: Principles and applications* (2nd ed.). Boston, MA: Allyn & Bacon.

Kaufman, L., & Rousseeuw, P. (1990). *Finding groups in data: An introduction to cluster analysis.* New York, NY: Wiley.

Mirkin, B. (2011). *Core concepts in data analysis: Summarization, correlation and visualization.* New York, NY: Springer.

National Governors Association. (2015). *Governors roster 2010: Governor's political affiliations & terms of office.* Retrieved from http://www.nga.org/files/live/sites/NGA/files/pdf/GOVLIST2010.PDF.

US Census Bureau. (2015). *Composition of Congress by politician party.* Retrieved from http://www.census.gov/compendia/statab/2011/tables/11s0404.pdf.

CHAPTER 6

# Empirical Analysis Part 2 Result and Findings: Empirical Example of Predicting the Demand for Life Insurance by Using the Dynamic Systemic Framework

**Abstract** In this chapter, an empirical example of research will be shown. By following the Part 1, the result and findings are described.

**Keywords** Nonlinear systemic analysis · Artificial neural network · Cluster analysis · Prediction

## 6.1 Analysis Procedure

The reporting of the statistical analyses is as follows: (a) descriptive analysis for understanding the general features of total observations used in the logistic model and artificial neural network (ANN) model; (b) cluster analysis used to divide observations into specific demographic groups; (c) splitting of the dataset into two categories (i.e., training dataset for estimation and test dataset for prediction); (d) logistic estimations used to find significant influential variables on the demand for life insurance; (e) logistic predictions in order to determine the efficiency of logistic estimations predictions; (f) ANN estimations used to find the order of influential variables on the demand for life insurance; and (g) ANN predictions in order to determine the efficiency of earlier ANN estimations. In order to accomplish the analysis procedure, appropriate statistical programs (i.e., STATA 12 and R Studio) were utilized.

© The Author(s) 2020

W. Heo, *The Demand for Life Insurance*,
https://doi.org/10.1007/978-3-030-36903-3_6

As explained in previous chapters, the main purposes of the study involved (a) comparing influential variables on the demand for life insurance based on two estimation methods (i.e., linear estimation and non-linear estimation) and (b) comparing the prediction power between the two estimations. For the analysis of linear estimation, logistic estimation was selected. With linear estimation, there are diverse analysis alternatives, such as ordinary least squares (OLS) estimation. The main reason for selecting logistic estimation/prediction instead of OLS was the feature of the dependent variables (i.e., life insurance status). As explained in the previous chapter, life insurance status was coded as three categories: (a) dropped life insurance between 2008 and 2012, (b) no change of possession status between 2008 and 2012, and (c) purchased life insurance between 2008 and 2012. Each category had its own probability of the number of respondents in the category. This means that influential variables (i.e., independent variables) influence each respondent's probability of belonging to one of the three categories. Logistic analysis is an efficient method to find probability of group membership, whereas OLS is efficient for finding the marginal effect of independent variables on a continuous dependent variable. Therefore, logistic analysis for linear estimation was used in this study instead of OLS analysis.

In terms of testing the prediction power of both analyses (i.e., logistic and ANN), root mean of square error (RMSE) was used. The function to calculate RMSE is shown below:

$$\text{RMSE} = \sqrt{\left(\frac{\left(P - \hat{P}\right)^2}{n - 1}\right)} \tag{6.1}$$

where $P$ denotes the observed probability of belonging to each category (i.e., dropped life insurance, no change of life insurance, and purchased life insurance). $P$-hat is the predicted probability by logistic prediction or ANN prediction, and $n$ is the total observation of each cluster. As the function shows, RMSE is calculated from the difference between observed probability and predicted probability. Therefore, a smaller RMSE means a more efficient prediction of probability.

## 6.2 Observations

The total sample of the study was 4680. Following the theoretical framework of the study, Tables 6.1, 6.2, and 6.3 show descriptive information for the sample by each characteristic (i.e., individual characteristics, family characteristics, and characteristics from the macro- and microenvironment).

**Table 6.1** Descriptive table for observations, individual characteristics

| *Variables* | n *(%)* | *Mean (SD)* |
|---|---|---|
| Education | | |
| Less than or equal to high school | 428 (9.15) | |
| College level | 3349 (71.56) | |
| Graduate or professional | 903 (19.29) | |
| Training | | |
| Have additional training | 592 (12.65) | |
| No additional training | 4088 (87.35) | |
| Interest in health | | |
| (0 = Never concerned; 5 = Always concerned) | | 3.27 (1.38) |
| Activities for health | | |
| (Frequency per week) | | 9.12 (17.30) |
| Activity against health | | |
| (Cans/glasses of alcohol last month) | | 1.41 (1.87) |
| Experience of family member's death | | |
| (Frequency in the past) | | .86 (1.08) |
| Sadness | | |
| Rarely | 3545 (75.75) | |
| Some | 744 (15.90) | |
| Occasionally | 232 (4.96) | |
| Most | 159 (3.40) | |
| Depression | | |
| Rarely | 3666 (78.33) | |
| Some | 617 (13.18) | |
| Occasionally | 224 (4.79) | |
| Most | 173 (3.70) | |
| Risk aversion | | |
| Lowest | 628 (13.42) | |
| Low | 355 (7.59) | |
| High | 1074 (22.95) | |
| Highest | 2623 (56.05) | |
| Self-esteem | | |
| (Lowest = 5; Highest = 30) | | 23.70 (4.38) |

*Note* $N = 4680$

**Table 6.2** Descriptive table for observations, family characteristics

| *Variables* | n *(%)* | *Mean (SD)* |
|---|---|---|
| Number of family members | | 2.84 (1.44) |
| Number of children | | 1.10 (1.45) |
| Marital status | | |
| Married | 2799 (59.81) | |
| Not married | 1881 (40.19) | |
| Marital history (Number of marriages) | | 1.04 (.90) |
| Total family income | | $69,662 (75,861) |
| Monetary assets | | $24,019 (118,085) |
| Bonds | | $3377 (42,149) |
| Debt status | | |
| In debt | 576 (12.31) | |
| Break even | 832 (17.78) | |
| Leftover assets | 3272 (69.91) | |
| Debt in credit card | | |
| Credit card debt | 2718 (58.08) | |
| No credit card debt | 1962 (41.92) | |
| Health insurance | | |
| Covered by health insurance | 3959 (84.59) | |
| Not covered by health insurance | 721 (15.41) | |
| Governmental assistance as income | | $573.69 (2360.21) |
| Ethnic background | | |
| White | 2413 (51.56) | |
| African-American | 1388 (29.66) | |
| Hispanic | 849 (18.14) | |
| Asian | 10 (.21) | |
| Native Hawaiian or Pacific Islander | 4 (.09) | |
| American Indian or Alaska native | 31 (.66) | |
| Others | 22 (.47) | |
| Region | | |
| Northeast | 679 (14.51) | |
| North central | 1135 (24.25) | |
| South | 1966 (42.01) | |
| West | 900 (19.23) | |
| Gender | | |
| Male | 2164 (46.24) | |
| Female | 2516 (53.76) | |
| Urbanization | | |
| Not in SMSA | 315 (6.73) | |
| SMSA but not central city | 2695 (57.59) | |
| SMSA in central city | 1492 (31.88) | |
| SMSA but central city not known | 178 (3.80) | |

*Note* $N=4680$

**Table 6.3** Descriptive table for observations, macro- and microenvironment

| *Variables* | n *(%)* | *Mean (SD)* |
|---|---|---|
| Job stability | | |
| (Number of different jobs in the past) | | 11.87 (6.78) |
| Tenure | | |
| (Number of weeks) | | 513.86 (465.34) |
| Class of worker | | |
| Government | 865 (18.48) | |
| Private for-profit company | 2392 (51.11) | |
| Non-profit organization | 366 (7.82) | |
| Self-employed | 406 (8.68) | |
| Family business | 37 (.79) | |
| Not categorized | 614 (13.12) | |
| Spouse working status | | |
| (Number of working weeks) | | 26.81 (24.94) |
| Type of residence | | |
| Living in own house | 4484 (95.81) | |
| Living in rented house | 196 (4.19) | |
| Mobility | | |
| Not moving | 45 (.86) | |
| Moving | 4635 (99.04) | |
| Community involvement | | |
| Participating | 1174 (25.09) | |
| Not participating | 3506 (74.91) | |
| Religious activities | | |
| Not at all | 464 (9.91) | |
| Several times during a year | 959 (20.49) | |
| About once a month | 599 (12.80) | |
| Two or three times a month | 415 (8.87) | |
| About once a week | 1093 (23.35) | |
| More than once a week | 1150 (24.57) | |
| Cultural norm | | |
| (1 = Very liberal; 25 = Very conservative) | | 13.74 (3.14) |
| Belonging to religion community | | |
| Roman Catholic | 2631 (56.22) | |
| Protestant Christian | 1159 (24.76) | |
| Jewish | 30 (.64) | |
| Other | 372 (7.95) | |
| No religion | 488 (10.43) | |
| Political trend | | |
| (Majority Republicans) | | 43.60 (11.74) |
| Social welfare rate of an area | | |
| (Welfare beneficiaries overall) | | 12.45 (.01) |
| Economic difficulties | | |
| (1 = Hard; 4 = Not hard) | | 1.97 (.74) |
| Unemployment weeks | | 3.16 (10.63) |

*Note* $N = 4680$

As shown in Table 6.1, most respondents reported an intermediate education level (72% at college level), but the rate of additional training was low (13%). Most respondents did not report severe sadness (76% rarely) or depression (78% rarely). Self-esteem was 23.70 out of 30. Based on the results for psychological characteristics (i.e., sadness, depression, and self-esteem), the majority of the sample was found not to be skewed toward any serious mental issues. In addition to mental health, around 80% of the sample showed high or the highest risk aversion. Most respondents experienced a death in the family approximately one time (0.86) in the past.

In terms of individual characteristics about health, respondents reported an intermediate level of health interest with a mean value of 3.27 (1 = never concerned and 5 = always concerned). Health activities, including vigorous or light activities, were close to seven per week, which implies that a large proportion of respondents engaged in healthy activities more than one time per day. In addition, the reported average number of cans or glasses of alcohol per month was only 1.41. Therefore, it is possible to surmise that most respondents were concerned about health issues and engaged in generally healthy lifestyles.

Table 6.2 shows the family characteristics of respondents. In terms of demographic features, the average number of family members was 2.84, and the average number of children was 1.10. Over half (60%) were married and most respondents had 1.04 marriage experiences. This implies that the average respondent had one marriage. The number of female respondents (54%) was slightly more than males. The majority of the respondents were either White or African-American (82%). In descending order, by number of respondents, the regions were south, north central, west, and northeast. Around 93% of respondents lived in or near a metropolitan area.

In the case of family finances, total family income for the given survey years was $69,662.3 with a standard deviation of $75,861.08. This implies that respondents' incomes varied. Average monetary assets were $24,019. These assets support the fluctuation of family income since monetary assets are relatively much smaller than family income. The liquidity of family income was possibly linked with the small amount of monetary assets. Average bond values were $3377. Debt status was financially favorable since respondent assets were sufficient to pay down debt. An interesting point is that many respondents (58%) reported that they had credit card debt. This implies that same respondents used their credit cards for daily life spending tool.

Table 6.3 describes the microenvironmental and macroenvironmental characteristics of respondents. In terms of employment, half of respondents worked for a private company (51%). Spouse working weeks were not as high as respondents tenured weeks. Specifically, tenure weeks of respondents were measured during the past five years and up to five jobs. Therefore, the total number of weeks could possibly range over 270 weeks (54 weeks for 5 years). However, the standard deviation of tenure weeks was 465.34 weeks. This suggests that many of the respondents' job stability fluctuated. This was linked with the high number of jobs (i.e., 11.87 jobs in the past). In addition, the average unemployment weeks over all areas were 3.16, with a standard deviation of 10.63.

In the case of residential features, most respondents (96%) owned their houses. In addition, most respondents (99%) had not moved out of their state in the past. Residential features were linked with (a) their high rate of belonging to any type of religious community (90%) and (b) their high frequency of participating in a religious activity (70% at least once a month). An interesting aspect of the data was that community involvement (25%) was lower than religious activity. It is possible to summarize that religious worship was more motivating than civil activities.

## 6.3 Sub-sampling by Cluster Analysis

As seen in the descriptive tables, respondents exhibited diverse features in various characteristic categories. One estimation and prediction for the whole sample was not reasonable to use with these diverse characteristics. Specifically, in order to improve the prediction power, sub-sampling was used to increase efficiency for statistical estimations. In the study, hierarchical clustering with Ward's method was utilized. Using many criteria variables to divide sub-samples makes it difficult to specify sub-samples (Mirkin, 2011). The criteria variables for clustering were selected from the socio-demographic variables (i.e., education level, marital status, family size, monetary assets, and gender). The sub-sampling results are shown in Table 6.4 for categorical criteria variables. Table 6.5 shows results for the continuous criteria variables.

In the case of education, among Clusters A and B, there were not large variations in average education level. However, Clusters C, D, and E showed higher education rates compared to Clusters A and B. For marital status, in Cluster A, only half of the respondents were married. Cluster B showed a higher number of married respondents.

**Table 6.4** Sub-sampling by cluster analysis, categorical demographics

| | *Total (N = 4680)* | *Cluster A (n = 1587)* | *Cluster B (n = 2350)* | *Cluster C (n = 631)* | *Cluster D (n = 93)* | *Cluster E (n = 19)* |
|---|---|---|---|---|---|---|
| | N *(%)* | n *(%)* | n *(%)* | n *(%)* | n *(%)* | n *(%)* |
| Education | | | | | | |
| Less than high school | 428 (9) | 155 (9) | 221 (9) | 47 (7) | 5 (6) | 0 (0) |
| College level | 3349 (72) | 1136 (72) | 1663 (71) | 464 (74) | 71 (76) | 15 (79) |
| Graduate level | 903 (19) | 296 (19) | 466 (20) | 120 (19) | 17 (18) | 4 (21) |
| Marital status | | | | | | |
| Married | 2799 (60) | 814 (51) | 1437 (61) | 465 (74) | 67 (72) | 16 (84) |
| Gender | | | | | | |
| Male | 2164 (46) | 517 (33) | 1145 (49) | 421 (67) | 67 (72) | 14 (74) |

*Note* N = 4680

**Table 6.5** Sub-sampling by cluster analysis, continuous demographics

| | *Total (N = 4680)* | *Cluster A (n = 1587)* | *Cluster B (n = 2350)* | *Cluster C (n = 631)* | *Cluster D (n = 93)* | *Cluster E (n = 19)* |
|---|---|---|---|---|---|---|
| | *Mean (SD)* | *Mean (SD)* | *Mean (SD)* | *Mean (SD)* | *Mean (SD)* | *Mean (SD)* |
| Family size | 2.85 (1.45) | 2.78 (1.49) | 2.83 (1.43) | 3.01 (1.38) | 3.20 (1.54) | 3.15 (1.46) |
| Monetary asset | $24,019 (118,085) | $13,430 (57,743) | $20,666 (99,820) | $41,744 (86,499) | $91,746 (181,804) | $403,079 (1,184,073) |

*Note* N = 4680

Clusters C, D, and E had higher rates of married respondents. By alphabetical order, each cluster had an increasing rate of married respondents. Similar to marital status, gender rates among clusters were in alphabetical order. Cluster A had the lowest rate of male respondents. Cluster E had the highest rate of males. Correspondingly, alphabetical order of the clusters showed increases in family size and monetary assets as well. Cluster A had the smallest number of family members and monetary assets. Cluster E had the largest number of family members and monetary assets.

Each cluster can be described as follows:

(a) Cluster A represents lower income single females who have low monetary assets;
(b) Cluster B is representative of the entire sample since all information is close to the overall average;

(c) Cluster C includes married males who have high education and high monetary assets;
(d) Clusters D and E are all married males who have extremely high education and monetary assets. Clusters D and E are representative of the top 1% of the sample.

The clusters demonstrate the reality of US socio-demographic profiles. For instance, males generally have more opportunity to be wealthy (Lyons, Neelakantan, & Scherpf, 2008). Social circumstances for females may be harsher than the social circumstances for males (Fonseca, Mullen, Zamarro, & Zissimopoulos, 2012). Cluster A, with low wealth females, is conceivably reflecting this reality. Likewise, married males with stable socioeconomic surroundings may become more wealthy like those in Cluster C. Clusters D and E represent the top 1% of wealthy people. These clusters reflect the wealth inequality in the United States (Saez & Zucman, 2014). As a result, by combining socio-demographic features together, all clusters found in the study are generalizable to the United States as a whole.

It is important to note, however, that Clusters D and E did not have large sample sizes (i.e., 93 and 19, respectively). For the next part of the study (i.e., multinomial logistic estimation and prediction, and ANN estimation and prediction), these sample sizes were not large enough to execute the analyses. Therefore, from this point forward, Clusters D and E were excluded from the logistic and ANN estimations and predictions.

## 6.4 Split of Data

The purposes of the study were to (a) compare influential variables on the demand for life insurance and (b) compare the prediction power between the two estimations. In order to address these issues, with three Clusters (i.e., Clusters A, B, and C), the dataset was divided into two datasets: a training dataset for estimations and a testing dataset for predictions. Results from the first estimation provide a list of influential variables, as well as the odds ratio (i.e., logistic estimation) and weight power (i.e., ANN estimation). By conducting the estimation, it was possible to find influential factors on the demand for life insurance. In terms of prediction with the testing dataset, the model was used to predict each respondent's probability of dropping/no change/purchasing life insurance. After the prediction of probabilities, the actual probability

**Table 6.6** Split of observations into training set and testing set (Clusters A, B, and C only)

| | *Training set* | *Test set* | *Total* |
|---|---|---|---|
| Cluster A | 800 | 787 | 1587 |
| Cluster B | 1164 | 1186 | 2350 |
| Cluster C | 314 | 317 | 631 |
| Total | 2278 | 2290 | 4568 |

of dropping/no change/purchasing life insurance of the testing dataset was compared to each respondent. As explained previously, comparing RMSE scores is one way to compare predicted probability with observed actual probability.

In order to divide the sample into two datasets, random sampling was conducted on each cluster. Table 6.6 shows the result of the random sampling procedure on each cluster. The dividing ratio was 50% to 50%. Therefore, the total respondents in the training dataset were 2278, excluding Clusters D and E. The other 2290 were in the testing dataset. Specifically, in the training dataset, the numbers in Clusters A, B, and C were 800, 1164, and 314, respectively. Similarly, the numbers in Clusters A, B, and C in the testing dataset were 787, 1186, and 317, respectively.

## 6.5 Influential Variables Found by Logistic Estimations Among the Three Clusters

In order to investigate the influential variables' odds ratios for dropping/purchasing life insurance, one of the three categories in the dependent variable (i.e., no change of life insurance) was selected as the reference group. Table 6.7 shows the results of multinomial logistic estimation for the sample in Cluster A.

Compared to the no change category (i.e., reference group), four influential variables had a significant effect on dropping life insurance between 2008 and 2012. First, monetary assets and tenure weeks showed a significant impact on dropping life insurance. However, the actual odds ratio was close to 1.00, with a standard deviation of 0.00. The numbers mean that there was no actual impact of the two variables. In other words, the two influential variables were significant, but there was no meaningful effect. Second, frequency of religious activities had a negative impact on dropping life insurance. Someone who attended

**Table 6.7** Multinomial logistic estimations in training model by using half of Cluster A

| | *Odds ratio* | *SE* | *95% CI* |
|---|---|---|---|
| *Drop life insurance* | | | |
| Education | 1.06 | 0.28 | [0.63, 1.79] |
| Training | 0.88 | 0.42 | [0.34, 2.26] |
| Health interest | 1.22 | 0.13 | [0.98, 1.51] |
| Healthy activity | 1.00 | 0.01 | [0.98, 1.02] |
| Average drinks | 0.99 | 0.08 | [0.83, 1.17] |
| Death experience | 1.00 | 0.12 | [0.78, 1.26] |
| Sadness | 1.01 | 0.25 | [0.62, 1.63] |
| Depression | 0.73 | 0.19 | [0.44, 1.20] |
| Risk aversion | 0.91 | 0.12 | [0.71, 1.18] |
| Self-esteem | 1.01 | 0.03 | [0.94, 1.07] |
| Family size | 1.12 | 0.14 | [0.88, 1.42] |
| Marital status | 0.81 | 0.38 | [0.32, 2.05] |
| Marital history | 0.91 | 0.13 | [0.68, 1.21] |
| Number of children | 0.86 | 0.12 | [0.65, 1.14] |
| Total family income | 1.00 | 0.00 | [1.00, 1.00] |
| Governmental income | 1.00 | 0.00 | [1.00, 1.00] |
| Monetary assets | 1.00* | 0.00 | [1.00, 1.00] |
| Debt status | 1.50 | 0.34 | [0.96, 2.33] |
| Bonds | 1.00 | 0.00 | [1.00, 1.00] |
| Credit debt | 1.12 | 0.33 | [0.62, 2.01] |
| Health insurance | 0.71 | 0.25 | [0.36, 1.40] |
| Ethnic | | | |
| African-American | 0.80 | 0.30 | [0.38, 1.67] |
| Hispanic | 0.49 | 0.22 | [0.20, 1.20] |
| Gender (Male) | 0.86 | 0.36 | [0.38, 1.96] |
| Urbanization | | | |
| Not in SMSA | 0.63 | 0.43 | [0.16, 2.42] |
| SMSA but not central city | 1.48 | 0.49 | [0.78, 2.82] |
| SMSA but not known | 0.80 | 0.66 | [0.16, 3.99] |
| Region | | | |
| North central | 0.73 | 0.37 | [0.27, 1.97] |
| South | 0.78 | 0.37 | [0.31, 1.99] |
| West | 0.92 | 0.48 | [0.33, 2.54] |
| Job history | 1.02 | 0.02 | [0.97, 1.06] |
| Tenure | 1.00* | 0.00 | [1.00, 1.00] |
| Job class | | | |
| Government | 0.49 | 0.25 | [0.18, 1.31] |
| Non-profit organization | 0.83 | 0.53 | [0.24, 2.90] |
| Self-employed | 0.49 | 0.25 | [0.18, 1.34] |
| Family business | 0.00 | 0.00 | [0.00, 0.00] |

(continued)

**Table 6.7** (continued)

| | *Odds ratio* | *SE* | *95% CI* |
|---|---|---|---|
| Not known | 1.35 | 0.53 | [0.63, 2.93] |
| Spouse working weeks | 1.00 | 0.01 | [0.99, 1.02] |
| Moving | 0.00 | 0.00 | [0.00, 0.00] |
| House ownership | 0.87 | 0.53 | [0.26, 2.89] |
| Religious activities | 0.84* | 0.07 | [0.71, 0.99] |
| Community involvements | 0.98 | 0.33 | [0.51, 1.91] |
| Religion | | | |
| Catholic | 0.76 | 0.31 | [0.34, 1.68] |
| Jewish | 0.00 | 0.00 | [0.00, 0.00] |
| Other | 2.54* | 1.06 | [1.12, 5.75] |
| No religion | 0.48 | 0.31 | [0.14, 1.72] |
| Family conservativeness | 0.98 | 0.04 | [0.90, 1.06] |
| Unemployment weeks | 1.01 | 0.01 | [0.99, 1.02] |
| Economic difficulties | 0.85 | 0.17 | [0.58, 1.27] |
| Constant | 0.18 | 0.29 | [0.01, 4.20] |
| **Reference level = No change in ownership of life insurance** | | | |
| *Purchase life insurance* | | | |
| Education | 0.85 | 0.21 | [0.52, 1.39] |
| Training | 0.47 | 0.27 | [0.15, 1.44] |
| Health interest | 1.04 | 0.10 | [0.86, 1.26] |
| Healthy activity | 1.00 | 0.01 | [0.98, 1.02] |
| Average drinks | 1.07 | 0.06 | [0.96, 1.20] |
| Death experience | 1.09 | 0.12 | [0.88, 1.35] |
| Sadness | 1.08 | 0.22 | [0.73, 1.61] |
| Depression | 1.17 | 0.23 | [0.79, 1.73] |
| Risk aversion | 1.07 | 0.14 | [0.83, 1.37] |
| Self-esteem | 1.00 | 0.03 | [0.94, 1.06] |
| Family size | 1.10 | 0.11 | [0.90, 1.35] |
| Marital status | 0.82 | 0.34 | [0.36, 1.86] |
| Marital history | 0.93 | 0.13 | [0.70, 1.22] |
| Number of children | 0.97 | 0.11 | [0.79, 1.20] |
| Total family income | 1.00 | 0.00 | [1.00, 1.00] |
| Governmental income | 1.00 | 0.00 | [1.00, 1.00] |
| Monetary assets | 1.00 | 0.00 | [1.00, 1.00] |
| Debt status | 1.61* | 0.32 | [1.10, 2.37] |
| Bonds | 1.00 | 0.00 | [1.00, 1.00] |
| Credit debt | 1.57 | 0.45 | [0.90, 2.75] |
| Health insurance | 0.84 | 0.26 | [0.45, 1.54] |
| Ethnic | | | |
| African-American | 2.06* | 0.76 | [1.00, 4.23] |
| Hispanic | 1.11 | 0.45 | [0.50, 2.47] |
| Gender (Male) | 0.60 | 0.24 | [0.28, 1.30] |

(continued)

**Table 6.7** (continued)

| | *Odds ratio* | *SE* | *95% CI* |
|---|---|---|---|
| Urbanization | | | |
| Not in SMSA | 1.22 | 0.65 | [0.43, 3.48] |
| SMSA but not central city | 1.28 | 0.39 | [0.71, 2.32] |
| SMSA but not known | 1.05 | 0.85 | [0.22, 5.10] |
| Region | | | |
| North central | 0.50 | 0.23 | [0.20, 1.22] |
| South | 0.53 | 0.22 | [0.23, 1.22] |
| West | 0.42 | 0.21 | [0.16, 1.10] |
| Job history | 1.00 | 0.02 | [0.96, 1.05] |
| Tenure | 1.00 | 0.00 | [1.00, 1.00] |
| Job class | | | |
| Government | 0.69 | 0.32 | [0.27, 1.71] |
| Non-profit organization | 1.06 | 0.67 | [0.31, 3.62] |
| Self-employed | 0.81 | 0.37 | [0.33, 1.98] |
| Family business | 0.00 | 0.00 | [0.00, .] |
| Not known | 0.70 | 0.25 | [0.35, 1.39] |
| Spouse working weeks | 1.01 | 0.01 | [1.00, 1.03] |
| Moving | 6.26** | 3.88 | [1.85, 21.11] |
| House ownership | 0.93 | 0.51 | [0.32, 2.74] |
| Religious activities | 0.94 | 0.08 | [0.80, 1.11] |
| Community involvements | 0.50 | 0.19 | [0.24, 1.05] |
| Religion | | | |
| Catholic | 0.91 | 0.34 | [0.44, 1.90] |
| Jewish | 0.00 | 0.01 | [0.00, 0.00] |
| Other | 0.43 | 0.25 | [0.14, 1.33] |
| No religion | 0.83 | 0.43 | [0.30, 2.29] |
| Family conservativeness | 1.06 | 0.04 | [0.98, 1.16] |
| Unemployment weeks | 0.99 | 0.01 | [0.97, 1.01] |
| Economic difficulties | 0.84 | 0.16 | [0.58, 1.21] |
| Constant | 0.08 | 0.12 | [0.00, 1.56] |

*Note* $n=800$. Pseudo $R^2=.1163$; $\chi^2=115.42$. $^*p<.05$; $^{**}p<.01$; $^{***}p<.001$. Political trends and welfare rates were omitted because of their multicollinearity with other macroenvironmental variables. Reference groups for categorical variables were: Whites, females, SMSA central city, northeast, governmental workers, and protestant Christians

more frequent religious activities in Cluster A was less likely to drop his/her life insurance. Interestingly, other religions showed a greater likelihood of dropping (OR=2.54, $p<.05$) when compared to the protestant Christian religion (i.e., reference group in religion). Therefore, it is possible that religious activity amplifies the ownership of life insurance but same religious affiliations lead to a reduction in the ownership of life insurance for lower income and wealth families.

On the other hand, compared to no change in having life insurance, three variables had a significant impact on purchasing life insurance. First, debt status was positively related to the ownership of life insurance (OR=1.61, $p<.05$). Remembering that debt status was reverse coded (in debt=−1, break even=0, and leftover assets=1), people who had less debt in Cluster A were more likely to purchase life insurance. The finding is consistent with the previous literature that wealth or net worth is positively associated with the ownership of life insurance (Eisenhauer & Halek, 1999; Hau, 2000; Heo, Grable, & Chatterjee, 2013). Second, African-American respondents in Cluster A showed a higher likelihood of purchasing life insurance (OR=2.06, $p<.05$) compared to White respondents (i.e., reference group). Considering education levels as a proxy for human capital, it is reasonable to conclude that African-American households within Cluster A insured a higher proportion of their human capital than White households. Third, respondents who had moved (i.e., move=1, not move=0) showed a higher likelihood of purchasing life insurance (OR=6.26, $p<.01$). Mobility was linked with stability of residence; as such, the probability of purchasing life insurance was significantly higher than 1.00.

Table 6.8 shows the results from the multinomial logistic estimation for the sample in Cluster B. As shown in the table, the significant influential variables associated with dropping/purchasing life insurance were totally different than Cluster A. This means that influential variables have different impacts on the demand for life insurance based on differences in socio-demographic features.

Five influential variables had a significant impact on dropping life insurance in Cluster B: (a) marital status, (b) marital history, (c) urbanization near metropolis (i.e., SMSA but not in central city), (d) job class (i.e., family business), and (e) economic difficulties. First, living with a spouse resulted in a higher likelihood of dropping life insurance (OR=2.69 $p<.01$). As mentioned in the previous chapters, marital status is a controversial variable. Some researchers (e.g., Lewis, 1989) have found that marital status is significantly and positively associated with the ownership of life insurance. But others (e.g., Burnett & Palmer, 1984; Hammond, Houston, & Melander, 1967; Mantis & Farmer, 1968) have noted that marital status is negatively or non-significantly associated with the ownership of life insurance. At least in Cluster B, the finding from the logistic estimation supports the notion that marital status is significantly and negatively related to the ownership of life insurance. Second, marital

**Table 6.8** Multinomial logistic estimations in training model by using half of Cluster B

| | *Odds ratio* | *SE* | *95% CI* |
|---|---|---|---|
| *Drop life insurance* | | | |
| Education | 0.95 | 0.18 | [0.66, 1.37] |
| Training | 1.11 | 0.33 | [0.62, 1.98] |
| Health interest | 1.01 | 0.08 | [0.87, 1.17] |
| Healthy activity | 1.00 | 0.01 | [0.99, 1.02] |
| Average drinks | 1.00 | 0.06 | [0.89, 1.12] |
| Death experience | 0.88 | 0.10 | [0.70, 1.11] |
| Sadness | 0.97 | 0.20 | [0.65, 1.45] |
| Depression | 1.21 | 0.25 | [0.81, 1.81] |
| Risk aversion | 0.87 | 0.08 | [0.72, 1.04] |
| Self-esteem | 1.02 | 0.02 | [0.97, 1.07] |
| Family size | 0.94 | 0.08 | [0.79, 1.11] |
| Marital status | 2.69** | 0.88 | [1.42, 5.10] |
| Marital history | 0.73* | 0.10 | [0.56, 0.96] |
| Number of children | 1.11 | 0.13 | [0.89, 1.39] |
| Total family income | 1.00 | 0.00 | [1.00, 1.00] |
| Governmental income | 1.00 | 0.00 | [1.00, 1.00] |
| Monetary assets | 1.00 | 0.00 | [1.00, 1.00] |
| Debt status | 1.09 | 0.18 | [0.79, 1.49] |
| Bonds | 1.00 | 0.00 | [1.00, 1.00] |
| Credit debt | 0.85 | 0.19 | [0.55, 1.30] |
| Health insurance | 1.64 | 0.66 | [0.75, 3.59] |
| Ethnic | | | |
| African-American | 1.41 | 0.39 | [0.82, 2.42] |
| Hispanic | 1.51 | 0.46 | [0.83, 2.76] |
| Gender (Male) | 1.29 | 0.42 | [0.68, 2.44] |
| Urbanization | | | |
| Not in SMSA | 0.59 | 0.32 | [0.20, 1.72] |
| SMSA but not central city | 1.82* | 0.43 | [1.14, 2.89] |
| SMSA but not known | 0.48 | 0.37 | [0.10, 2.20] |
| Region | | | |
| North central | 1.36 | 0.46 | [0.69, 2.65] |
| South | 1.22 | 0.40 | [0.64, 2.32] |
| West | 1.30 | 0.49 | [0.62, 2.73] |
| Job history | 0.99 | 0.02 | [0.96, 1.03] |
| Tenure | 1.00 | 0.00 | [1.00, 1.00] |
| Job class | | | |
| Government | 0.78 | 0.21 | [0.46, 1.32] |
| Non-profit organization | 1.13 | 0.42 | [0.54, 2.34] |
| Self-employed | 1.26 | 0.51 | [0.57, 2.80] |
| Family business | 17.68*** | 15.74 | [3.09, 101.23] |
| Not known | 0.00 | 0.00 | [0.00, 0.00] |
| Spouse working weeks | 1.00 | 0.01 | [0.99, 1.01] |
| Moving | 0.00 | 0.00 | [0.00, 0.00] |

(continued)

**Table 6.8** (continued)

| | *Odds ratio* | *SE* | *95% CI* |
|---|---|---|---|
| House ownership | 1.14e+05 | 2.48e+08 | [0.00, 0.00] |
| Religious activities | 1.02 | 0.07 | [0.89, 1.17] |
| Community involvements | 0.92 | 0.22 | [0.58, 1.47] |
| Religion | | | |
| Catholic | 0.62 | 0.18 | [0.35, 1.07] |
| Jewish | 0.00 | 0.00 | [0.00, 0.00] |
| Other | 0.67 | 0.29 | [0.28, 1.56] |
| No religion | 1.49 | 0.48 | [0.79, 2.80] |
| Family conservativeness | 1.02 | 0.04 | [0.95, 1.09] |
| Unemployment weeks | 1.00 | 0.03 | [0.95, 1.05] |
| Economic difficulties | 0.70* | 0.10 | [0.53, 0.94] |
| Constant | 0.00 | 0.00 | [0.00, 0.00] |
| **Reference level = No change in ownership of life insurance** | | | |
| *Purchase life insurance* | | | |
| Education | 0.99 | 0.19 | [0.68, 1.46] |
| Training | 1.47 | 0.39 | [0.88, 2.47] |
| Health interest | 1.10 | 0.09 | [0.94, 1.28] |
| Healthy activity | 1.01 | 0.01 | [1.00, 1.02] |
| Average drinks | 0.93 | 0.06 | [0.82, 1.05] |
| Death experience | 1.19 | 0.12 | [0.97, 1.45] |
| Sadness | 0.88 | 0.19 | [0.58, 1.34] |
| Depression | 0.89 | 0.20 | [0.58, 1.37] |
| Risk aversion | 1.20 | 0.14 | [0.95, 1.52] |
| Self-esteem | 0.97 | 0.02 | [0.92, 1.02] |
| Family size | 1.04 | 0.09 | [0.88, 1.24] |
| Marital status | 1.50 | 0.49 | [0.79, 2.85] |
| Marital history | 0.99 | 0.13 | [0.77, 1.29] |
| Number of children | 0.84 | 0.10 | [0.67, 1.05] |
| Total family income | 1.00 | 0.00 | [1.00, 1.00] |
| Governmental income | 1.00 | 0.00 | [1.00, 1.00] |
| Monetary assets | 1.00 | 0.00 | [1.00, 1.00] |
| Debt status | 0.98 | 0.16 | [0.71, 1.36] |
| Bonds | 1.00 | 0.00 | [1.00, 1.00] |
| Credit debt | 1.62* | 0.38 | [1.03, 2.56] |
| Health insurance | 0.80 | 0.31 | [0.38, 1.69] |
| Ethnic | | | |
| African-American | 2.81*** | 0.79 | [1.62, 4.88] |
| Hispanic | 1.73 | 0.55 | [0.93, 3.21] |
| Gender (Male) | 0.79 | 0.24 | [0.44, 1.43] |
| Urbanization | | | |
| Not in SMSA | 1.84 | 0.80 | [0.79, 4.31] |
| SMSA but not central city | 1.97** | 0.48 | [1.22, 3.19] |
| SMSA but not known | 0.52 | 0.40 | [0.11, 2.36] |
| Region | | | |
| North central | 0.47* | 0.15 | [0.25, 0.89] |
| South | 0.56* | 0.16 | [0.32, 0.98] |

(continued)

**Table 6.8** (continued)

| | *Odds ratio* | *SE* | *95% CI* |
|---|---|---|---|
| West | 0.49* | 0.18 | [0.24, 0.99] |
| Job history | 0.97 | 0.02 | [0.93, 1.01] |
| Tenure | 1.00 | 0.00 | [1.00, 1.00] |
| Job class | | | |
| Government | 1.69* | 0.41 | [1.05, 2.72] |
| Non-profit organization | 2.31* | 0.80 | [1.17, 4.57] |
| Self-employed | 0.95 | 0.49 | [0.34, 2.62] |
| Family business | 3.60 | 4.53 | [0.31, 42.35] |
| Not known | 1.71 | 1.50 | [0.31, 9.58] |
| Spouse working weeks | 1.00 | 0.01 | [0.99, 1.01] |
| Moving | 0.00 | 0.00 | [0.00, 0.00] |
| House ownership | 3.68 | 3.98 | [0.44, 30.63] |
| Religious activities | 0.98 | 0.07 | [0.86, 1.12] |
| Community involvements | 0.85* | 0.21 | [0.52, 1.39] |
| Religion | | | |
| Catholic | 0.92 | 0.27 | [0.52, 1.63] |
| Jewish | 0.85 | 0.96 | [0.09, 7.82] |
| Other | 1.06 | 0.40 | [0.50, 2.22] |
| No religion | 1.07 | 0.41 | [0.51, 2.27] |
| Family conservativeness | 0.92* | 0.03 | [0.86, 0.99] |
| Unemployment weeks | 0.99 | 0.03 | [0.93, 1.04] |
| Economic difficulties | 0.90 | 0.13 | [0.68, 1.19] |
| Constant | 0.11 | 0.18 | [0.00, 2.74] |

*Note* $n=1164$. Pseudo $R^2=.1043$. $\chi^2=167.70$ ($p<.001$). *$p<.05$; **$p<.01$; ***$p<.001$. Political trends and welfare rates were omitted because of their multicollinearity with other macroenvironmental variables. Reference groups for categorical variables were: Whites, females, SMSA central city, northeast, governmental workers, and protestant Christians

history was negatively associated with dropping life insurance (OR=.73, $p<.05$). Respondents who reported more marriages were less likely to drop life insurance. Considering that life insurance, as used in this study, was delimited to cash value life insurance, the financial purpose of having life insurance seems to be related to the finding. Third, respondents who lived in a metropolitan area, but not in a central city, had a higher likelihood of dropping life insurance (OR=1.82, $p<.05$). This suggests that urbanization is associated with the ownership of life insurance. Fourth, respondents with family businesses in Cluster B showed an extremely high likelihood of dropping life insurance (OR=17.68, $p<.001$). It may be that the wealth associated with a family business can be used to financially compensate others when losing a family member. It may also indicate lack of diversification among business owners. Finally, economic difficulties were negatively associated with dropping life insurance

(OR=.70, $p<.05$). Some may think that cash value life insurance is a form of investment and drop coverage in economic hard times.

In the case of purchasing life insurance in Cluster B, there were seven significant variables: (a) credit card debt, (b) African-American, (c) urbanization (i.e., SMSA but not in central city), (d) region (i.e., north central, south, and west), (e) job class (i.e., worker for government, and worker for non-profit organization), (f) community involvement, and (g) family conservativeness. First, credit card debt had a positive association with purchasing life insurance (OR=1.62, $p<.05$). Second, as with Cluster A, African-Americans showed a positive association with purchasing life insurance (OR=2.81, $p<.001$). Third, as with dropping life insurance in Cluster B, respondents who lived in a metropolitan area but not in the central city were more likely to purchase life insurance (OR=1.97, $p<.01$). This shows the polarized ownership status of life insurance in urban areas. Fourth, region was a significant influential variable on the ownership of life insurance. Compared to the reference group (i.e., northeast area), respondents in all other areas (i.e., north central, south, and west) had a significantly smaller likelihood of purchasing life insurance (OR=.47, $p<.05$; OR=.56, $p<.05$; OR=.49, $p<.05$, respectively). Fifth, government workers and those employed by non-profit organizations were more likely to purchase life insurance (OR=1.69, $p<.05$; OR=2.31, $p<.05$, respectively) compared to private company workers (i.e., reference group). Sixth, respondents who participated in more community activities were less likely to purchase life insurance (OR=.85, $p<.05$). Finally, family attitudes toward conservativeness were negatively associated with purchasing life insurance (OR=.92, $p<.05$).

Table 6.9 shows the result from the multinomial logistic estimation for those in Cluster C. As there were different influential variables for those in Clusters A and B, it was not surprising that the significant influential variables associated with dropping/purchasing life insurance in Cluster C were different than in Cluster A or Cluster B. This implies, again, that influential variables have different impacts on demand for life insurance based on different socio-demographic groups.

Six influential variables were shown to have a significant impact on dropping life insurance in Cluster C: (a) average drinking, (b) depression, (c) marital history, (d) tenure weeks, (e) job class (i.e., working for the government), and (f) religion (i.e., Catholic). First, respondents with higher frequencies of negative health activities (i.e., high frequencies in average drinking) reported a greater likelihood of dropping life insurance

**Table 6.9** Multinomial logistic estimations in training model by using half of Cluster C

| | *Odds ratio* | *SE* | *95% CI* |
|---|---|---|---|
| *Drop life insurance* | | | |
| Education | 1.04 | 0.46 | [0.44, 2.47] |
| Training | 0.87 | 0.50 | [0.28, 2.69] |
| Health interest | 1.08 | 0.18 | [0.78, 1.50] |
| Healthy activity | 1.00 | 0.02 | [0.96, 1.05] |
| Average drinks | 1.49* | 0.25 | [1.07, 2.06] |
| Death experience | 0.74 | 0.23 | [0.40, 1.34] |
| Sadness | 0.55 | 0.27 | [0.21, 1.44] |
| Depression | 3.09* | 1.49 | [1.21, 7.94] |
| Risk aversion | 1.17 | 0.24 | [0.79, 1.74] |
| Self-esteem | 1.04 | 0.06 | [0.94, 1.16] |
| Family size | 0.73 | 0.16 | [0.48, 1.14] |
| Marital status | 3.25 | 2.82 | [0.59, 17.79] |
| Marital history | 0.44* | 0.17 | [0.21, 0.94] |
| Number of children | 0.83 | 0.33 | [0.38, 1.81] |
| Total family income | 1.00 | 0.00 | [1.00, 1.00] |
| Governmental income | 1.00 | 0.00 | [1.00, 1.00] |
| Monetary assets | 1.00 | 0.00 | [1.00, 1.00] |
| Debt status | 0.90 | 0.36 | [0.41, 1.99] |
| Bonds | 1.00 | 0.00 | [1.00, 1.00] |
| Credit debt | 0.81 | 0.44 | [0.28, 2.36] |
| Health insurance | 5.11e+05 | 1.74e+09 | [0.00, 0.00] |
| Ethnic | | | |
| African-American | 2.57 | 1.46 | [0.84, 7.82] |
| Hispanic | 2.46 | 1.76 | [0.60, 9.99] |
| Gender (Male) | 0.71 | 0.58 | [0.14, 3.57] |
| Urbanization | | | |
| Not in SMSA | 1.08 | 1.17 | [0.13, 9.01] |
| SMSA but not central | 1.22 | 0.64 | [0.44, 3.41] |
| SMSA but not known | 0.80 | 0.84 | [0.10, 6.29] |
| Region | | | |
| North central | 0.72 | 0.50 | [0.18, 2.85] |
| South | 0.72 | 0.49 | [0.19, 2.74] |
| West | 0.61 | 0.47 | [0.14, 2.73] |
| Job history | 1.08 | 0.05 | [1.00, 1.18] |
| Tenure | 1.00* | 0.00 | [1.00, 1.00] |
| Job class | | | |
| Government | 0.25* | 0.17 | [0.06, 0.97] |
| Non-profit org. | 0.49 | 0.33 | [0.13, 1.83] |
| Self-employed | 0.80 | 0.60 | [0.18, 3.49] |
| Spouse working weeks | 1.01 | 0.01 | [0.98, 1.03] |
| Religious activities | 0.83 | 0.13 | [0.61, 1.13] |
| Community involvements | 1.83 | 0.83 | [0.75, 4.46] |

(continued)

**Table 6.9** (continued)

| | *Odds ratio* | *SE* | *95% CI* |
|---|---|---|---|
| Religion | | | |
| Catholic | 0.25* | 0.17 | [0.07, 0.92] |
| Jewish | 0.00 | 0.00 | [0.00, .] |
| Other | 1.22 | 1.17 | [0.19, 7.97] |
| No religion | 2.92 | 1.94 | [0.79, 10.75] |
| Family conservativeness | 1.04 | 0.08 | [0.90, 1.21] |
| Unemployment weeks | 0.00 | 0.00 | [0.00, 0.00] |
| Economic difficulties | 1.12 | 0.35 | [0.61, 2.05] |
| Constant | 0.00 | 0.00 | [0.00, 0.00] |
| **Reference level = No change in ownership of life insurance** | | | |
| *Purchase life insurance* | | | |
| Education | 0.43 | 0.27 | [0.12, 1.47] |
| Training | 1.94 | 1.29 | [0.53, 7.14] |
| Health interest | 0.75 | 0.18 | [0.47, 1.20] |
| Healthy activity | 0.94 | 0.05 | [0.84, 1.05] |
| Average drinks | 1.13 | 0.25 | [0.73, 1.74] |
| Death experience | 1.51 | 0.52 | [0.77, 2.99] |
| Sadness | 0.31 | 0.37 | [0.03, 3.34] |
| Depression | 0.76 | 0.81 | [0.09, 6.13] |
| Risk aversion | 1.78 | 0.62 | [0.89, 3.54] |
| Self-esteem | 1.07 | 0.09 | [0.91, 1.25] |
| Family size | 0.69 | 0.20 | [0.39, 1.21] |
| Marital status | 22.68* | 33.49 | [1.25, 409.99] |
| Marital history | 0.45 | 0.26 | [0.15, 1.38] |
| Number of children | 2.88 | 1.72 | [0.89, 9.31] |
| Total family income | 1.00 | 0.00 | [1.00, 1.00] |
| Governmental income | 0.99 | 12.53 | [0.00, 6.46e + 08] |
| Monetary assets | 1.00 | 0.00 | [1.00, 1.00] |
| Debt status | 9.14 | 14.79 | [0.38, 218.30] |
| Bonds | 1.00 | 0.00 | [1.00, 1.00] |
| Credit debt | 2.20 | 1.92 | [0.40, 12.10] |
| Health insurance | 0.20 | 0.30 | [0.01, 3.66] |
| Ethnic | | | |
| African-American | 2.90 | 2.37 | [0.59, 14.37] |
| Hispanic | 0.99 | 0.96 | [0.15, 6.61] |
| Gender (Male) | 10.97 | 16.03 | [0.63, 192.15] |
| Urbanization | | | |
| Not in SMSA | 1.79 | 2.39 | [0.13, 24.52] |
| SMSA but not central | 0.43 | 0.33 | [0.10, 1.91] |
| SMSA but not known | 6.95 | 8.48 | [0.63, 76.01] |
| Region | | | |
| North central | 0.47 | 0.38 | [0.10, 2.31] |
| South | 0.08* | 0.08 | [0.01, 0.50] |
| West | 0.03* | 0.04 | [0.00, 0.67] |

(continued)

**Table 6.9** (continued)

| | *Odds ratio* | *SE* | *95% CI* |
|---|---|---|---|
| Job history | 1.01 | 0.06 | [0.90, 1.13] |
| Tenure | 1.00 | 0.00 | [1.00, 1.00] |
| Job class | | | |
| Government | 2.62 | 2.29 | [0.47, 14.49] |
| Non-profit org. | 1.08 | 1.05 | [0.16, 7.33] |
| Self-employed | 3.04 | 3.29 | [0.36, 25.35] |
| Spouse working weeks | 1.00 | 0.02 | [0.96, 1.05] |
| Religious activities | 1.01 | 0.23 | [0.65, 1.57] |
| Community involvements | 2.03 | 1.29 | [0.58, 7.08] |
| Religion | | | |
| Catholic | 0.39 | 0.31 | [0.08, 1.82] |
| Jewish | 0.00 | 0.00 | [0.00, 0.00] |
| Other | 0.49 | 0.72 | [0.03, 8.77] |
| No religion | 1.21 | 1.45 | [0.11, 12.78] |
| Family conservativeness | 0.91 | 0.10 | [0.74, 1.12] |
| Unemployment weeks | 1.07 | 0.12 | [0.85, 1.34] |
| Economic difficulties | 1.03 | 0.50 | [0.40, 2.65] |
| Constant | 0.00 | 0.00 | [0.00, 0.00] |

*Note* $n=314$. Pseudo $R^2=.2965$; $\chi^2=122.24$. $^*p<.05$; $^{**}p<.01$; $^{***}p<.001$. Political trends and welfare rates were omitted because of their multicollinearity with other macroenvironmental variables. Family business and not-known in job class were omitted because of the small number of observations. Mobility and homeownership were omitted because of the small number of rent-house observations. Reference groups for categorical variables were: Whites, females, SMSA central city, northeast, governmental workers, and protestant Christians

(OR=1.49, $p<.05$). Second, depression level (0=rarely, 3=all the time) showed a significantly positive association with dropping life insurance (OR=3.09, $p<.05$). This means that depressed people were more likely to drop their life insurance. Third, as in Cluster B, marital history was negatively associated with dropping life insurance (OR=.44, $p<.05$). Fourth, like the case with Cluster A, tenure weeks of respondents in Cluster C showed a significant impact on the ownership of life insurance (OR=1.00, $p<.05$). However, the odds ratio was 1.00, which means 0% chance in dropping life insurance. While the variable was statistically significant, it did not have an actual impact on the ownership of life insurance. Fifth, working for the government was negatively associated with dropping life insurance (OR=.25, $p<.05$). Finally, those who were Catholic showed a negative likelihood of dropping life insurance (OR=.25, $p<.05$).

**Table 6.10** Significant influential variables from logistic model (Clusters A, B, and C)

| | *Cluster A* | *Cluster B* | *Cluster C* |
|---|---|---|---|
| Drop | Monetary assets (+)<br>Tenure (+)<br>Religious activity (−)<br>Religion: Other (+) | Marital status (+)<br>Marital history (−)<br>Urbanization: SMSA but not city (+)<br>Job class: Family business (+)<br>Econ. difficulties (−) | Average drink (+)<br>Marital history (−)<br>Depression (+)<br>Tenure (+)<br>Job class: Government (−)<br>Religion: Catholic (−) |
| Purchase | Debt status (+)<br>Ethnic: African-American (+)<br>Moving (+) | Credit debt (−)<br>Ethnic: African-American (+)<br>Urbanization: SMSA but not city (+)<br>Region:<br>North central (−)<br>South (−)<br>West (−)<br>Job class:<br>Government (+)<br>Non-profit org. (+)<br>Family conserve. (−) | Marital status (+)<br>Region:<br>South (−)<br>West (−) |

*Note* Reference group in the multinomial logistic model: no change of life insurance ownership

A few variables were found to influence the decision to purchase life insurance. The variables were marital status and regions (i.e., south and west). First, in Cluster C, the finding from the logistic estimation indicated that marital status was positively associated with purchasing life insurance (OR=22.68, $p<.05$). Considering that Cluster C included relatively wealthy respondents with more family members, an existence of main beneficiary (i.e., spouse) may be the important factor related to purchasing life insurance. Second, region (i.e., south and west) showed a lower likelihood of purchasing life insurance compared to the northeast area (OR=.08, $p<.05$; OR=.03, $p<.05$, respectively). This was the same as in Cluster B. This implies that there is a certain regional trend related to purchasing life insurance.

Table 6.10 summarizes the significant influential variables associated with Clusters A, B, and C. In summary, the three clusters had different socio-demographic features. Most respondents in Cluster A were low wealth and single females. Most respondents in Cluster B were males with typical families. Most respondents in Cluster C were males who were relatively wealthy with big families. Based on the different socio-demographic features of the three clusters, it was not unexpected to find varying influences of variables.

Cluster A had a low wealth feature. Other variables in Cluster A were related to a person's financial position (e.g., monetary assets, tenure, and debt status). In the case of Cluster A, financial variables appear to influence the ownership of life insurance. In the case of Cluster B, the cluster represented the profiles of average consumers. The factors found in Cluster B contained most of the variables found in Clusters A and C. In Cluster C, the most frequent variables were job-related factors (e.g., job history and tenure) and health-related variables (e.g., health insurance and average drinks). Considering that Cluster C was relatively comprised of wealthy people with large families, the variables seem to be reasonable description.

## 6.6 Probability Prediction Using Logistic Estimations Among the Three Clusters

By using the odds ratios found with the multinomial logistic estimations among the three clusters (see Tables 6.7, 6.8, and 6.9) and the multinomial logistic function (see function [5.4] in Chapter 5), it was possible to predict the probability of belonging to one of the three categories of the dependent variable: (a) probability of belonging to group who dropped life insurance, (b) probability of belonging to group who did not change their life insurance ownership, and (c) probability of belonging to group who purchased life insurance (see Table 6.11).

**Table 6.11** Probability prediction comparison with observed probability, multinomial logistic model

| | *Probability* | | | *Error* | | |
|---|---|---|---|---|---|---|
| | *Pr(Dr)* | *Pr(NC)* | *Pr(Pur)* | *Pr(Dr)* | *Pr(NC)* | *Pr(Pur)* |
| Observed Probability | | | | | | |
| Probability in Cluster A | .0966 | .8170 | .0864 | – | – | – |
| Probability in Cluster B | .1096 | .7858 | .1046 | – | – | – |
| Probability in Cluster C | .1073 | .8170 | .0757 | – | – | – |
| Predicted Probability | | | | | | |
| Mean Pr. of Cluster A | .0897 | .8078 | .1025 | .0069 | .0092 | .0161 |
| Mean Pr. of Cluster B | .1157 | .7608 | .1396 | .0061 | .0250 | .0350 |
| Mean Pr. of Cluster C | .1178 | .8088 | .0734 | .0105 | .0082 | .0023 |

*Note* $n = 2290$ in test dataset. Pr(Dr): probability of dropping pre-existing life insurance; Pr(NC): probability of no change of life insurance; and Pr(Pur): probability of purchasing new life insurance. Error is reported as absolute number of difference between observed probability and predicted probability (i.e., |observed probability – predicted probability|)

**Table 6.12** RMSE comparison among clusters, logistic with testing dataset

| | *Cluster A* (n = *787*) | *Cluster B* (n = *1186*) | *Cluster C* (n = *317*) |
|---|---|---|---|
| Drop life insurance | .0972 | .0969 | .1593 |
| No change in life insurance | .1247 | .1418 | .2104 |
| Purchase life insurance | .0863 | .1169 | .1490 |

In the process, another dataset (i.e., testing dataset $n=2290$) was utilized for predictions among the three clusters. As shown in Table 6.11, the probabilities of belonging to any of three categories (i.e., dropping, no change, and purchasing) were compared with actual probabilities from the testing dataset (i.e., observed probability). The observed probability from the testing dataset was calculated from observed frequencies of the three categories of the dependent variable. A larger error number ($=|$predicted probability $-$ observed probability$|$) means less effective prediction for a respondent. On the other hand, a smaller error number denotes a more accurate prediction of one of the three categories of the dependent variable.

Based on the calculation of the error between the predicted probability and the observed probability, it was possible to calculate RMSE. As explained at the beginning of previous, RMSE is a way of indicating how close a prediction is to the observed value. Table 6.12 shows the final RMSE that was calculated using the multinomial logistic estimation/prediction procedure. In terms of clusters, the prediction level for Cluster A was the most robust among the three clusters. In terms of three categories of dependent variable, prediction power for no change in life insurance was less robust than the other two categories. However, between the other two categories, it was hard to differentiate which one was more powerful. For instance, the prediction for purchasing coverage was more powerful than the prediction for dropping coverage in the case of Cluster A, but the prediction for dropping coverage was more powerful than the prediction for purchasing coverage in the case of Cluster B. The result was that no change in life insurance showed the lowest prediction power compared to the other two categories.

## 6.7 Influential Variables Found Using ANN Estimations Among the Three Clusters

Before finalizing a list of influential variables on the demand for life insurance, an appropriate statistical formation of ANN estimation had to be established. ANN estimation differs by the number of hidden layers and decay weight. A hidden layer is the conceptual station where all influential factors are interdependently interacting (see function [2.1], function [2.2], and Fig. 2.2 in Chapter 2). The purpose of the existence of a hidden layer is to amalgamate all covariance among all variables in a model in order to improve the prediction power. Different numbers of hidden layers cause different prediction power. Therefore, the first step is to find the optimized number of hidden layers. A specific decay weight is needed when using ANN modeling because of over-fitting problems with ANN. Without a specific decay weight, ANN estimation reduces bias, which results in over-fitting of the dataset. Over-fitting means that the ANN estimation is precisely optimized to a specific dataset but not generalized to other datasets. Therefore, a specific decay weight should be selected and used with ANN estimation.

Figures 6.1 and 6.2 show the prediction power changed by the number of hidden layers and decay weights among three clusters. The case with a decay weight of 0.001 shows a more powerful and stable error rate for prediction in the test dataset. Specifically, the error rate of prediction in Clusters B and C fluctuated more with a decay weight of 0.1 than with a decay weight of 0.001. Therefore, the optimized number of 0.001 decay weight was selected in the study. In terms of the number of hidden layers, in all three clusters, more numbers of hidden layers increased the error rates in both decay weights of 0.1 and 0.001. Therefore, one hidden layer was chosen as the optimized number for the study. By using the optimized number of hidden layers and the decay weight, the ANN estimations indicated different influential variables on the demand for life insurance among the three clusters.

Table 6.13 shows the influential variables on the demand for life insurance in Cluster A. The weight value denotes the prominence of influential variables associated with the probability of falling into one of the three categories of the dependent variable: (a) dropping life insurance, (b) no change in ownership of life insurance, and (c) purchasing

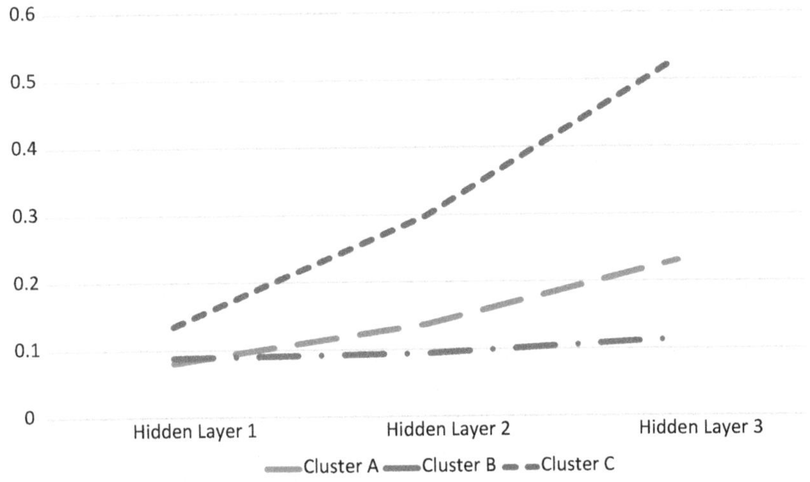


**Fig. 6.1** Prediction error rate by different numbers of hidden layers in ANN model (Clusters A, B, and C) with decay weight of 0.001

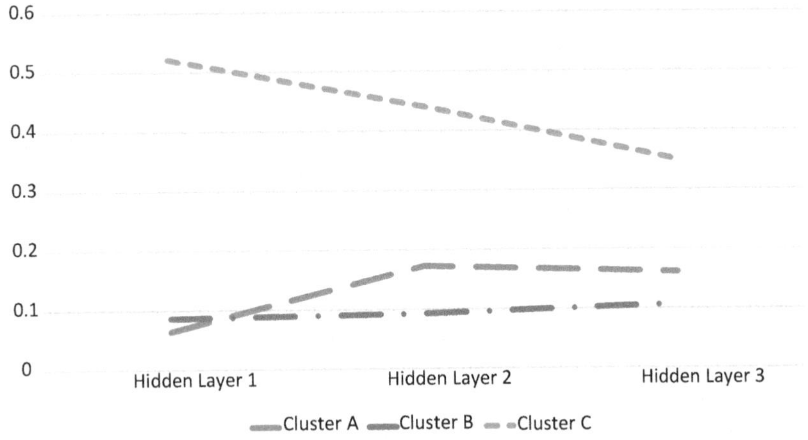


**Fig. 6.2** Prediction error rate by different numbers of hidden layers in ANN model (Clusters A, B, and C) with decay weight of 0.1

**Table 6.13** ANN estimations in training model by using half of Cluster A

| *No.* | *Dropping life insurance* | | *Purchasing life insurance* | |
|---|---|---|---|---|
| | *Input variables* | *Weight value* | *Input variables* | *Weight value* |
| 1 | Ethnic: Hispanic | 7.89 | Religion: Other religion | 9.65 |
| 2 | Bond | 5.45 | Ethnic: White | 8.85 |
| 3 | Job history | 5.05 | Self-esteem | 6.64 |
| 4 | Job: Not known | 4.71 | Mobility | 5.59 |
| 5 | Urb.: Not SMSA | 4.65 | Region: West | 4.71 |
| 6 | Marital history | 4.52 | Governmental income | 4.64 |
| 7 | Region: West | 3.84 | Number of children | 3.65 |
| 8 | Depression | 3.30 | Urb.: SMSA but not city | 3.29 |
| 9 | Sadness | 2.52 | Unemployment | 3.24 |
| 10 | Job: Self-employed | 2.51 | Job history | 3.17 |
| 11 | Ethnic: White | 2.23 | Religion: No religion | 3.01 |
| 12 | Religion: Jewish | 2.10 | Job: Self-employed | 2.60 |
| 13 | Urb.: SMSA city | 1.69 | Health insurance | 2.52 |
| 14 | Religion: No religion | 1.61 | Family income | 2.36 |
| 15 | Male | 1.56 | Sadness | 2.34 |
| 16 | Job: Government worker | 1.55 | Political trend | 2.05 |
| 17 | Education | 1.34 | Tenure | 1.74 |
| 18 | Training | 1.28 | Job: Not known | 1.53 |
| 19 | Credit card | 1.23 | Religion: Jewish | 1.39 |
| 20 | Average drink | 0.89 | Marital history | 1.30 |
| 21 | Community involvement | 0.76 | Job: Government worker | 1.13 |
| 22 | Death experience | 0.54 | Job: Family business | 1.10 |
| 23 | Risk aversion | 0.38 | Monetary assets | 0.68 |
| 24 | Religion: Protestant | 0.28 | Region: North central | 0.67 |
| 25 | Political trend | 0.14 | Community involvement | 0.62 |
| 26 | Region: North central | −0.06 | Male | 0.38 |
| 27 | Family size | −0.15 | Family conservativeness | 0.17 |
| 28 | Religious activity | −0.45 | Depression | −0.23 |
| 29 | Self-esteem | −0.66 | Urb.: SMSA city | −0.43 |
| 30 | Religion: Other religion | −0.81 | Economic difficulty | −0.46 |
| 31 | Ethnic: African-American | −1.14 | Healthy activity | −0.56 |
| 32 | Healthy activity | −1.22 | Job: Private company | −0.60 |
| 33 | Governmental income | −1.31 | Region: South | −0.87 |
| 34 | Job: Family business | −1.62 | Average drink | −1.33 |
| 35 | Region: South | −1.63 | Religious activity | −1.51 |
| 36 | Number of children | −1.71 | Religion: Catholic | −1.57 |
| 37 | Urb.: SMSA unknown | −1.71 | Education | −1.99 |
| 38 | Religion: Catholic | −1.79 | Welfare | −2.27 |
| 39 | Region: Northeast | −2.14 | Urb.: SMSA unknown | −3.17 |
| 40 | Family conservativeness | −2.38 | Urb.: Not in SMSA | −3.34 |
| 41 | Mobility | −2.51 | Ethnic: Hispanic | −4.08 |
| 42 | Welfare | −2.77 | Death experience | −4.13 |
| 43 | Health interest | −3.19 | Region: Northeast | −4.93 |

(continued)

**Table 6.13** (continued)

| *No.* | *Dropping life insurance* | | *Purchasing life insurance* | |
|---|---|---|---|---|
| | *Input variables* | *Weight value* | *Input variables* | *Weight value* |
| 44 | Urb.: SMSA but not city | −3.36 | Spouse working weeks | −4.93 |
| 45 | Job: Non-profit org. | −3.40 | Risk aversion | −5.20 |
| 46 | Job: Private company | −3.61 | Marital status | −5.26 |
| 47 | Economic difficulty | −3.62 | Health interest | −5.28 |
| 48 | House ownership | −4.15 | Ethnic: African-American | −5.35 |
| 49 | Monetary assets | −4.18 | Family size | −5.39 |
| 50 | Debt status | −4.55 | Job: Non-profit org. | −5.50 |
| 51 | Tenure | −4.89 | Religion: Protestant | −5.98 |
| 52 | Marital status | −5.43 | Bond | −6.37 |
| 53 | Spouse working weeks | −5.52 | Training | −6.61 |
| 54 | Unemployment | −5.97 | House ownership | −6.65 |
| 55 | Family income | −6.90 | Credit card | −7.39 |
| 56 | Health insurance | −7.54 | Debt status | −7.49 |

life insurance. Specifically, in Table 6.13, the probability of change in ownership of life insurance (i.e., dropping life insurance and purchasing life insurance) is shown. Larger numbers in weight value mean a bigger impact on one of the three categories of the dependent variable.

First, in terms of dropping life insurance, the top 10 variables that had a prominent impact on the dependent variable were: ethnicity (Hispanic), bond, job history, job class (not known), urbanization (not in SMSA), marital history, region (west), depression, sadness, and job class (self-employed). Race was a meaningful factor associated with dropping life insurance. For instance, being Hispanic showed the highest weight value linked with dropping life insurance and being White showed the eleventh highest weight value. This implies that African-Americans (weight value = −1.22) did not drop their life insurance at a rate less than Hispanics and Whites. Influential variables related to job (e.g., job history, unknown job class, and self-employed job class) showed high weight values for dropping life insurance (weight value = 5.05; weight value = 4.71; weight value = 2.51, respectively). Interestingly, psychological factors including depression and sadness showed high weight values (weight value = 3.30; weight value = 2.52, respectively). Considering that Cluster A mainly consisted of low wealth single females, it is reasonable to conclude that variables related to psychological features drove the prediction. Excluding the psychological factors, among the top 10 influential factors, cash in bonds showed the second highest weight value (5.45). This implies that cash in bonds worked as substitute for life insurance. Respondents who lived in a rural area (not SMSA) showed a greater propensity of dropping life insurance (weight value=4.65). More frequencies in marital history showed a high impact on dropping life insurance (weight value=4.52), and respondents who lived in the west area were more likely to drop their life insurance (weight value=3.84). In addition to the top 10 influential variables, being male was the fifteenth most prominent variable impacting the probability of being in one of the three categories of the dependent variable. This implies that switching gender from major (female) to minor (male) in Cluster A had a noteworthy impact on the probability of dropping life insurance.

Second, in terms of purchasing life insurance, the top 10 variables that had a prominent impact on the dependent variable were: religious community (other religion), ethnicity (White), self-esteem, mobility, region (west), governmental income, number of children, urbanization (SMSA but not in central city), unemployment, and job history. In Cluster A, respondents who dropped life insurance were influenced by relatively personal features (e.g., ethnicity, sadness, depression, job class, and job history). However, respondents who purchased life insurance were influenced by primarily external environmental features (e.g., religious community, mobility, region, urbanization, and unemployment). In other words, respondents in Cluster A dropped life insurance based on personal factors but purchased insurance by external factors. Interestingly, religious community affiliation showed the highest weight value (9.65, other religious community) and eleventh weight value (3.01, no religious community). This implies that mainstream religious communities including protestant Christian and Catholic were not as concerned with purchasing life insurance (weight value=−5.98; weight value=−1.57, respectively). Ethnicity (i.e., White) was found to affect the purchase of life insurance (weight value=8.85). Regarding that African-American had a negative weight value linked with dropping and purchasing (weight value=−1.14 and weight value=−5.35, respectively), White respondents showed more volatility of owning life insurance than African-Americans. Respondents who had a higher score in self-esteem showed more likelihood of purchasing life insurance (weight value=6.64). These with more frequencies of moving were found to be more likely to purchase life insurance (weight value=5.59). External factors like socioeconomic external environmental factors (i.e., governmental income and unemployment weeks) influenced the purchasing of life insurance (weight value=4.64; weight value=3.24, respectively). This finding implies that low wealth single females are strongly affected by social capital in terms of purchasing life insurance. Interestingly, the number of children in a household was shown to be an influential factor associated with purchasing life insurance (weight value=3.65). Living with someone who should be protected drove respondents in Cluster A to purchase life insurance. In terms of region, respondents living in the west showed a higher propensity to purchase life insurance (weight=4.71).

Table 6.14 shows the influential variable list for Cluster B. The top 10 variables that had a prominent impact on the probability of dropping life insurance were: job class (not known), death experience, bond, economic difficulty, ethnicity (White), depression, job history, male, region (west), and risk aversion. There were three factors from the individual system (i.e., psychological factors): death experience (weight value=9.08), depression (weight value=5.56), and risk aversion (weight value=3.22). Four factors were from the family system (i.e., family structure and family demographics): cash in bonds (weight value=6.40), White (weight value=5.59), male (weight value=4.35), and west (weight value=3.79). Two factors (i.e., physical habitat and social aspect) were from the microenvironmental system: job history (weight value=4.59) and not known job class (weight value=10.06). One factor was from the macroenvironmental system (i.e., economic environment): economic difficulty (weight value=6.35). Considering that Cluster B was mainly representative of average consumers from the sample, it is reasonable to conclude that the best prediction variables were related to all systems (i.e., individual, family, microenvironmental, and macroenvironmental system). In other words, similar to the conceptual approach within the systemic framework (see Fig. 2.1 in Chapter 2), diverse influential factors were found to interact within the same system and across different systems.

On the other hand, the top 10 variables that had impact on the probability of purchasing life insurance were: ethnicity (White), job class (family business), health insurance, job class (private company), religious community (other religion), region (west), job class (not known), spouse working weeks, urbanization (SMSA in city), and cash in bonds. Unlike the list for dropping life insurance in Cluster B, influential variables for purchasing life insurance were more closely related to the family and

**Table 6.14** ANN estimations in training model by using half of Cluster B

| *No.* | *Dropping life insurance* | | *Purchasing life insurance* | |
|---|---|---|---|---|
| | *Input variables* | *Weight value* | *Input variables* | *Weight value* |
| 1 | Job: Not known | 10.06 | Ethnic: White | 8.53 |
| 2 | Death experience | 9.08 | Job: Family business | 6.01 |
| 3 | Bond | 6.40 | Health insurance | 4.79 |
| 4 | Economic difficulty | 6.35 | Job: Private company | 4.46 |
| 5 | Ethnic: White | 5.59 | Religion: Other religion | 3.75 |
| 6 | Depression | 5.56 | Region: West | 3.68 |
| 7 | Job history | 4.59 | Job: Not known | 3.60 |
| 8 | Male | 4.35 | Spouse working weeks | 3.57 |
| 9 | Region: West | 3.79 | Urb.: SMSA city | 3.25 |
| 10 | Risk aversion | 3.22 | Bond | 1.92 |
| 11 | Unemployment | 2.98 | Sadness | 1.88 |
| 12 | Religion: Jewish | 2.90 | Region: North central | 1.85 |
| 13 | Marital history | 2.89 | Job history | 1.31 |
| 14 | Ethnic: Hispanic | 2.49 | Religion: Jewish | 1.29 |
| 15 | Family income | 2.41 | Economic difficulty | 1.19 |
| 16 | Training | 2.34 | Death experience | 0.94 |
| 17 | Urb.: SMSA unknown | 2.16 | Religious activity | 0.78 |
| 18 | Credit card | 2.00 | Political trend | 0.73 |
| 19 | Job: Self-employed | 1.97 | Male | 0.55 |
| 20 | Governmental income | 1.96 | Healthy activity | 0.49 |
| 21 | Urb.: SMSA city | 1.81 | Governmental income | 0.44 |
| 22 | Mobility | 1.65 | Community involvement | 0.05 |
| 23 | Job: Government worker | 1.45 | Urb.: SMSA unknown | −0.21 |
| 24 | Number of children | 1.37 | Mobility | −0.40 |
| 25 | Self-esteem | 1.21 | Religion: Catholic | −0.51 |
| 26 | Education | 0.85 | Unemployment | −0.70 |
| 27 | Religion: Protestant | 0.78 | Marital status | −0.75 |
| 28 | Sadness | 0.62 | Religion: No religion | −0.90 |
| 29 | Family size | 0.56 | Ethnic: Hispanic | −1.07 |
| 30 | Urb.: Not in SMSA | 0.47 | Self-esteem | −1.13 |
| 31 | Region: South | 0.30 | Family size | −1.24 |
| 32 | Religion: Catholic | 0.24 | Religion: Protestant | −1.25 |
| 33 | Average drink | 0.09 | Urb.: Not in SMSA | −1.55 |
| 34 | Region: Northeast | −0.14 | Number of children | −1.75 |
| 35 | Political trend | −0.32 | Family conservativeness | −1.76 |
| 36 | Religion: No religion | −0.41 | Tenure | −1.78 |
| 37 | Debt status | −0.65 | Region: South | −2.04 |
| 38 | Monetary assets | −1.09 | Welfare | −2.17 |
| 39 | Healthy activity | −1.57 | Urb.: SMSA but not city | −2.36 |
| 40 | Religious activity | −1.85 | Marital history | −2.41 |
| 41 | Job: Non-profit org. | −1.88 | Average drink | −2.78 |
| 42 | Religion: Other religion | −2.02 | Debt status | −2.86 |
| 43 | Community involvement | −2.30 | Family income | −2.94 |

(continued)

**Table 6.14** (continued)

| No. | Dropping life insurance | | Purchasing life insurance | |
|---|---|---|---|---|
| | *Input variables* | *Weight value* | *Input variables* | *Weight value* |
| 44 | Urb.: SMSA but not city | −2.61 | Monetary assets | −3.46 |
| 45 | Tenure | −2.62 | Region: Northeast | −3.50 |
| 46 | House ownership | −2.75 | House ownership | −3.53 |
| 47 | Job: Family business | −2.79 | Ethnic: African-American | −3.92 |
| 48 | Welfare | −3.64 | Job: Non-profit org. | −3.99 |
| 49 | Region: North central | −3.66 | Depression | −4.11 |
| 50 | Family conservativeness | −3.93 | Education | −4.17 |
| 51 | Health interest | −5.11 | Job: Government worker | −4.44 |
| 52 | Marital status | −6.44 | Job: Self-employed | −4.58 |
| 53 | Spouse working weeks | −7.23 | Risk aversion | −5.11 |
| 54 | Job: Private company | −7.69 | Training | −5.30 |
| 55 | Ethnic: African-American | −8.16 | Credit card | −5.48 |
| 56 | Health insurance | −9.36 | Health interest | −6.39 |

microenvironmental systems. In terms of the family system, five factors were listed as the top influential factors: White (weight value = 8.53), health insurance (weight value = 4.79), west (weight value = 3.68), cash in bonds (weight value = 1.92), and SMSA in city (weight value = 3.25). Four physical habitat factors from the microenvironmental system were listed on influential variables: family business worker (weight value = 6.01), private company worker (weight value = 4.46), not known job class (weight value = 3.60), and spouse working weeks (weight value = 3.57). This implies that family-centered factors drove the purchase of life insurance.

Table 6.15 shows the influential variable list associated with the demand for life insurance for those in Cluster C. The top 10 variables that had a prominent impact on the probability of dropping life insurance were: urbanization (not in SMSA), risk aversion, job class (not known), economic difficulty, male, religious community (Catholic), healthy activity, region (west), depression, and death experience. Among the top 10 influential variables, four factors were personal and psychological factors: risk aversion, healthy activity, depression, and death experience (weight value = 6.22; weight value = 5.12; weight value = 4.80; weight value = 4.46, respectively). These psychological and personal factors indicated that the lack of personal needs drove the decision to drop life insurance. For instance, wealthy consumers with high risk aversion and regular healthy activities may not believe that they need

**Table 6.15** ANN estimations in training model by using half of Cluster C

| *No.* | *Dropping life insurance* | | *Purchasing life insurance* | |
|---|---|---|---|---|
| | *Input variables* | *Weight value* | *Input variables* | *Weight value* |
| 1 | Urb.: Not in SMSA | 7.21 | Marital history | 8.51 |
| 2 | Risk aversion | 6.22 | Religion: Other religion | 8.08 |
| 3 | Job: Not known | 5.71 | Region: West | 6.28 |
| 4 | Economic difficulty | 5.66 | Ethnic: White | 6.01 |
| 5 | Male | 5.31 | Job history | 5.59 |
| 6 | Religion: Catholic | 5.27 | Job: Family business | 4.32 |
| 7 | Healthy activity | 5.12 | Job: Private company | 3.98 |
| 8 | Region: West | 4.99 | Urb.: SMSA city | 3.76 |
| 9 | Depression | 4.80 | Family income | 2.40 |
| 10 | Death experience | 4.46 | Sadness | 2.18 |
| 11 | Ethnic: Hispanic | 4.44 | Religious activity | 2.02 |
| 12 | Ethnic: White | 3.01 | Male | 1.96 |
| 13 | Monetary assets | 2.37 | Region: North central | 1.48 |
| 14 | Credit card | 2.23 | Self-esteem | 1.44 |
| 15 | Religion: Jewish | 2.19 | Governmental income | 1.43 |
| 16 | Debt status | 1.89 | Job: Non-profit org. | 1.37 |
| 17 | Number of children | 1.86 | Ethnic: Hispanic | 1.35 |
| 18 | Religion: Protestant | 1.42 | Family conservativeness | 1.05 |
| 19 | Region: Northeast | 1.26 | Tenure | 0.91 |
| 20 | Community involvement | 1.15 | Religion: Jewish | 0.81 |
| 21 | Job history | 1.12 | Healthy activity | 0.73 |
| 22 | Bond | 1.03 | Number of children | 0.60 |
| 23 | Religious activity | 0.82 | Unemployment | 0.58 |
| 24 | Marital status | 0.79 | Monetary assets | 0.42 |
| 25 | Self-esteem | 0.70 | House ownership | 0.40 |
| 26 | Urb.: SMSA but not city | 0.63 | Political trend | 0.37 |
| 27 | Unemployment | 0.57 | Religion: No religion | 0.17 |
| 28 | Health interest | 0.01 | Depression | 0.16 |
| 29 | Job: Government worker | −0.23 | Health insurance | 0.10 |
| 30 | Job: Non-profit org. | −0.35 | Job: Not known | −0.09 |
| 31 | Family size | −0.73 | Economic difficulty | −0.39 |
| 32 | Education | −0.84 | Credit card | −1.24 |
| 33 | Family income | −1.39 | Urb.: SMSA but not city | −1.25 |
| 34 | Marital history | −1.42 | Education | −1.71 |
| 35 | Sadness | −1.46 | Job: Self-employed | −2.09 |
| 36 | Job: Private company | −1.46 | Religion: Protestant | −2.21 |
| 37 | Job: Self-employed | −1.92 | Urb.: Not in SMSA | −2.26 |
| 38 | Region: North central | −2.00 | Marital status | −2.47 |
| 39 | Average drink | −2.28 | Religion: Catholic | −2.79 |
| 40 | Urb.: SMSA unknown | −2.78 | Urb.: SMSA unknown | −2.95 |
| 41 | Family conservativeness | −3.01 | Region: South | −3.09 |
| 42 | Region: South | −3.15 | Family size | −3.29 |
| 43 | Political trend | −3.22 | Community involvement | −3.47 |

(continued)

**Table 6.15** (continued)

| No. | Dropping life insurance | | Purchasing life insurance | |
|---|---|---|---|---|
| | *Input variables* | *Weight value* | *Input variables* | *Weight value* |
| 44 | Urb.: SMSA city | −3.37 | Welfare | −4.10 |
| 45 | Training | −3.44 | Death experience | −4.14 |
| 46 | Health insurance | −3.91 | Region: Northeast | −4.48 |
| 47 | Ethnic: African-American | −4.04 | Spouse working weeks | −4.74 |
| 48 | Governmental income | −4.12 | Training | −5.24 |
| 49 | Religion: No religion | −4.45 | Job: Government worker | −5.50 |
| 50 | Mobility | −4.51 | Health interest | −5.78 |
| 51 | Welfare | −5.48 | Debt status | −5.90 |
| 52 | Job: Family business | −5.50 | Bond | −6.07 |
| 53 | House ownership | −6.10 | Average drink | −6.53 |
| 54 | Religion: Other religion | −6.62 | Mobility | −7.44 |
| 55 | Tenure | −8.17 | Ethnic: African-American | −8.26 |
| 56 | Spouse working weeks | −9.79 | Risk aversion | −10.63 |

to invest their assets in cash value life insurance. This implies that their high wealth may act as a substitute function of cash value life insurance. The finding on economic difficulty supports the substitute association since economic difficulty drove some to drop life insurance (weight value = 5.66). In a harsh economic time, respondents in Cluster C were more likely to lean on their own wealth instead of owning life insurance. In addition, those with high depression and more frequencies of death experience may believe that they have less need for life insurance in their future. These findings suggest that respondents in Cluster C held a more pessimistic perspective on their future. An interesting point was that living in a rural area (not in SMSA) showed the highest weight value (7.21) on the decision to drop life insurance. This implies that wealthy consumers living in rural area were more likely independent by relying on their own support mechanisms. This might be related to the weight value (5.31) of males dropping life insurance. Rural males in the United States with high wealth might be more likely to be independent. In addition, mainstream religions, including Catholic and protestant Christian, showed high weight values on dropping life insurance (5.27 and 1.42, respectively).

In Cluster C, the top 10 influential variables associated with the purchase of life insurance were: marital history, religious community (other religion), region (west), ethnicity (White), job history, job class (family business), job class (private company), urbanization (SMSA city), family income, and sadness. The majority of these factors mainly belonged to the family system: marital history (weight value=8.51), west region (weight value=6.28), White (weight value=6.01), SMSA city (weight value=3.76), and family income (weight value=2.40). Specifically, variables that relate to financial independence in the future were found to impact life insurance decisions (e.g., job history, family income, working for family business, and working for private company). For instance, job history represented job stability, and it had high weight value (5.59). Family income was a representative index of family financial independence, and it had high weight value (2.40). Additionally, working for family business and private company showed high weight values (4.32 and 3.98, respectively). This implies that respondents in Cluster C considered life insurance as a hedge against unexpected events.

Another interesting point is that there were opposite influential factors (i.e., religious community and urbanization) between dropping and purchasing life insurance. In the case of dropping life insurance, mainstream religion affiliation (i.e., Catholic and protestant Christian) was linked with dropping life insurance. However, in terms of purchasing life insurance, being out of mainstream religion drove the purchase of life insurance. Other religion communities showed the second highest weight value (8.08), whereas mainstream religion community affiliation (Catholic and protestant Christian) showed a negative weight value (−2.79 and −2.21, respectively). As explained above, living in a rural area was strongly associated with dropping life insurance. Consistently, living in an urban area (living in SMSA) showed a positive impact on purchasing life insurance (weight value=3.76), but living in a rural area showed a negative impact on purchasing life insurance (weight value=−2.26).

## 6.8 Probability Prediction by Using ANN Estimations Among the Three Clusters

In order to predict the probability of belonging to one of the three categories of dependent variable (i.e., dropping life insurance, no change in life insurance, and purchasing life insurance), the same logistic procedure was utilized. By using the variable weights found with the ANN estimations among the three clusters (see Tables 6.13, 6.14, and 6.15) and the ANN function (see function [5.3] in Chapter 5), it was possible

**Table 6.16** Probability prediction comparison with observed probability, ANN model

| | *Probability* | | | *Error* | | |
|---|---|---|---|---|---|---|
| | *Pr(Dr)* | *Pr(NC)* | *Pr(Pur)* | *Pr(Dr)* | *Pr(NC)* | *Pr(Pur)* |
| Observed probability | | | | | | |
| Probability in Cluster A | .0966 | .8170 | .0864 | – | – | – |
| Probability in Cluster B | .1096 | .7858 | .1046 | – | – | – |
| Probability in Cluster C | .1073 | .8170 | .0757 | – | – | – |
| Predicted probability | | | | | | |
| Mean Pr. of Cluster A | .0857 | .8139 | .0922 | .0109 | .0031 | .0058 |
| Mean Pr. of Cluster B | .1160 | .7859 | .1008 | .0064 | .0001 | .0038 |
| Mean Pr. of Cluster C | .1161 | .7794 | .0974 | .0088 | .0379 | .0217 |

*Note* $n=2290$ in test dataset. Pr(Dr): probability of dropping pre-existing life insurance; Pr(NC): probability of no change in life insurance; and Pr(Pur): probability of purchasing new life insurance. Error is reported as absolute number of difference between observed probability and predicted probability (i.e., |observed probability – predicted probability|)

to predict the probability of belonging to one of the three categories of the dependent variable (see Table 6.16). In the process of predicting, another dataset (i.e., testing dataset, $n=2290$) was utilized for predictions among the three clusters. As shown in Table 6.17, probabilities of belonging to one of the three categories (i.e., dropping, no change, and purchasing) were compared with the actual probabilities from the testing dataset (i.e., observed probability). The observed probability from the testing dataset was calculated from the observed frequencies in the three categories of the dependent variable. Therefore, a larger error number (=|predicted probability – observed probability|) means a less effective prediction. On the other hand, a smaller error number denotes a more accurate prediction of belonging to one of the three categories of dependent variable.

**Table 6.17** RMSE comparison among clusters, ANN with testing dataset

| | *Cluster A* (n=*787*) | *Cluster B* (n=*1186*) | *Cluster C* (n=*317*) |
|---|---|---|---|
| Drop life insurance | .0490 | .0512 | .0450 |
| No change in life insurance | .0876 | .0795 | .0770 |
| Purchase life insurance | .0522 | .0452 | .0576 |

Based on the calculation of the error between the predicted probability and the observed probability, RMSE was utilized to compare the prediction power among the three clusters. Table 6.17 shows the final RMSE that was calculated by the ANN estimation/prediction procedure. In terms of the clusters, prediction levels for Clusters A and C were relatively more powerful than Cluster B. The prediction for average consumers in Cluster B was less powerful than Clusters A and C. This finding suggests that socio-demographic features are strongly related to the prediction level of the demand for life insurance. Specific groups like Clusters A and C showed more powerful prediction of life insurance demand but average consumers like those in Cluster C showed less powerful prediction of life insurance demand. In terms of the three categories of the dependent variable, the prediction power for the no change in life insurance group was less powerful than the other two categories. On the other hand, the prediction power for purchasing life insurance was the most powerful. This hints at the possibility that the reason for purchasing life insurance is more clear than the reason for dropping life insurance.

## 6.9 Influential Variables Comparison Between the Logistic and ANN

Tables 6.18 and 6.19 show the comparison between the significant variable lists found using the logistic estimation and the ANN estimation methods. In terms of the logistic estimation, variables with a significant level of $p < .05$ are listed in the tables. In the case of ANN estimation, the top 10 important variables are shown in the tables.

Looking at Tables 6.18 and 6.19, it is possible to conclude that there are two types of influential variables associated with the demand for life insurance: (a) variables with unique covariance found mainly using logistic estimation and (b) variables with shared covariance found mainly using ANN estimation. The unique covariance means the covariance is shared by only two variables, a specific independent variable and the dependent variable (e.g., a partial covariance shared only between religious activity and the demand for life insurance). In other words, the unique covariance is the source for calculating the regression coefficient, which is called the marginal effect. On the other hand, the shared covariance is the covariance shared by several other variables, as well as the

**Table 6.18** Dropping life insurance influential variable comparison between logistic and ANN estimations

| | *Cluster A* | | *Cluster B* | | *Cluster C* | |
|---|---|---|---|---|---|---|
| | *Logistic* | *ANN* | *Logistic* | *ANN* | *Logistic* | *ANN* |
| Common | | | Economic difficulty | | Religion: Catholic depression | |
| Separate | Monetary assets<br>Tenure weeks<br>Religious activity<br>Religion: Other | Ethnic: Hispanic<br>Bond<br>Job history<br>Job class: Not known<br>Urbanization: Not SMSA<br>Marital history<br>Region: West<br>Depression<br>Sadness<br>Job: Self-employed | Marital status<br>Marital history<br>Urbanization: SMSA but not city<br>Family business | Job class: Not known<br>Death experience<br>Bond<br>Ethnic: White<br>Depression<br>Job history<br>Male<br>Region: West<br>Risk aversion | Average drink<br>Marital history<br>Tenure<br>Government worker | Urbanization: Not in SMSA<br>Risk aversion<br>Job: Not known<br>Economic difficulty<br>Male<br>Healthy activity<br>Region: West<br>Death experience |

*Note* Logistic estimation: variables with significant level below .05 are listed on the table regardless of the significance level. ANN estimation: top 10 prominent variables are listed regardless of the weight order

**Table 6.19** Purchasing life insurance influential variable comparison between logistic and ANN estimations

| | *Cluster A* | | *Cluster B* | | *Cluster C* | |
|---|---|---|---|---|---|---|
| | *Logistic* | *ANN* | *Logistic* | *ANN* | *Logistic* | *ANN* |
| Common | Mobility | | Region: West | | Region: West | |
| Separate | Debt status<br>African-American | Religion: Other<br>Ethnic: White<br>Self-esteem<br>Region: West<br>Governmental income<br>Number of children<br>Urbanization: SMSA but not city<br>Unemp. weeks<br>Job history | Credit debt<br>African-American<br>Urbanization: SMSA but not city<br>Region:<br>North central<br>South<br>Government worker<br>Non-profit worker | Ethnic: White<br>Job class: Family business<br>Health insurance<br>Job class: Private company<br>Religion: Other<br>Job class: Not known<br>Spouse working weeks<br>Urbanization: SMSA city<br>Bond | Marital status<br>Region: South | Marital history<br>Religion: Other<br>Ethnic: White<br>Job history<br>Job class: Family business<br>Job class: Private company<br>Urbanization: SMSA city<br>Family income<br>Sadness |

*Note* Logistic estimation: variables with significant level below .05 are listed on the table regardless of the significance level. ANN estimation: top 10 prominent variables are listed regardless of the weight order dependent variable (e.g., a covariance shared among family size, spouse working weeks, health interest, and the demand for life insurance). In the general regression estimation, the shared covariance is automatically dropped by the statistical function. Therefore, the results are revealed as non-significant variables on the demand for life insurance even though the variables share covariance with the dependent variable.

In Cluster A, the logistic estimation and ANN estimation shared one common variable (i.e., mobility) in the case of purchasing life insurance. The common variable has both (a) unique covariance with the demand for life insurance and (b) shared covariance with other variables including the demand for life insurance. As Cluster A mainly consists of low wealth single females, it is reasonable to conclude that both estimations indicate that more frequent moving history drove the consumers to purchase life insurance as a protection tool. However, the most influential variables from the ANN estimation were different from that generated with the logistic estimations.

In the case of dropping life insurance, the top ranked variables found using ANN were: Hispanic, cash in bonds, job history, not known job class, rural area, marital history, west region, depression, sadness, and self-employed job class. These variables were totally different compared to the significant variables in the logistic estimations, which were: monetary assets, tenure weeks, religious activity, and other religious community. This means that four significant variables found by logistic estimation had marginal effect on the dropping life insurance. In other words, these four significant variables had unique covariance with dropping life insurance. However, these four significant variables did not have a large portion of shared covariance with the other influential variables associated with the dropping life insurance. The top ranked variables found using ANN showed larger a portion of shared covariance with other influential variables among those who dropped life insurance. This implies that the actual basic demand for life insurance could be influenced by the top ranked variables found using ANN estimation.

In terms of purchasing life insurance, the top ranked variables that emerged from the ANN procedure were: other religious community, White, self-esteem, west region, governmental income, number of children, rural area, unemployment weeks, and job history. These variables were differed from the findings using logistic estimation, which identified debt status and African-American. This means that just a few significant variables found by logistic estimation seem to be associated with the decision to purchase life insurance. However, beyond the marginal effect, there are more variables (e.g., other religious community, White, self-esteem, west region, governmental income, number of children, rural area, unemployment weeks, and job history) that appear to be associated with purchasing life insurance. The top ranked variables found using ANN showed a larger portion of shared covariance with other influential variables. This implies that the actual basic demand for life insurance could be influenced by the top ranked variables found using ANN.

In the case of Cluster B, there were two variables common to both the logistic and ANN estimations: economic difficulty on dropping life insurance and west region on purchasing life insurance. Considering that Cluster B represented average consumers in the United States, the common variables associated with dropping life insurance hint at the possibility that economic difficulty drives the life insurance decision-making process for these concerns. However, the common variables in Cluster B were not same as in Cluster A. This was caused by the different socio-demographic features of Clusters A and B. Since each had different socio-demographic features, the needs for life insurance are naturally different.

In the case of dropping life insurance in Cluster B, the top ranked variables found using ANN were: not known job class, death experience, cash in bonds, White, depression, job history, male, west region, and risk aversion. These variables, except economic difficulty, differed from significant variables identified in the logistic estimations: marital status, marital history, urban area, and family business worker. This means that four significant variables found using logistic estimation have a marginal effect on the dropping life insurance. On the other hand, the top ranked variables found using ANN show a larger portion of shared covariance with other influential variables. In terms of purchasing life insurance, the top ranked variables found using ANN were: White, family business workers, health insurance coverage, private company worker, other religious community, know known job class, spouse working weeks, urban area, and cash in bonds. These variables differed from the variable identified using logistic estimation: credit debt, African-American, urban area (not central city), north central region, south region, government worker, and non-profit organization worker. The significant variables were found to have marginal impact on the purchasing life insurance. However, beyond the marginal effect, there were more variables shown to be associated with purchasing life insurance using ANN estimations.

Finally, in the case of Cluster C, there were three variables common to both the logistic and ANN estimations: (a) depression, (b) Catholic religious community, and (b) west region. The common variables in Cluster C were not the same as in Clusters A and B. This was caused by the different socio-demographic features of Clusters A, B, and C. In the case of dropping life insurance in Cluster C, the top ranked variables found using ANN were: urban area (not in central city), risk aversion, economic difficulty, male, healthy activity, west region, and death experience. These variables differed from the significant variables found using logistic estimations: average drinking, marital history, tenure, and governmental worker. Top ranked variables found using ANN denote the basic influential variables associated with dropping life insurance. In contrast, significant variables found using logistic estimation symbolize marginal effects beyond the basic variable lists. In terms of purchasing life insurance, the top ranked variables found using ANN were: marital history, other religious community, White, job history, family business worker, private company worker, urban area, family income, and sadness. These variables differed from the findings using logistic estimation: marital status and south region. The significant variables were found to have marginal influences on the life insurance purchase decision. However, beyond the marginal effect, there were more variables shown to be associated with purchasing life insurance using ANN estimations.

## 6.10 Prediction Rate Comparison Between the Logistic and ANN Methods

Table 6.20 shows the comparison between the logistic prediction and the ANN prediction level by cluster. As explained above, RMSE was used to compare the prediction levels. Smaller numbers in RMSE mean smaller fluctuations in predicted probabilities in the testing dataset. Therefore, a smaller number represents a more accurate prediction of probability. As shown in Table 6.20, in all cases, the demand for life insurance (i.e., dropping, no change, and purchasing life insurance) probabilities predicted using ANN showed better performance. The main reason for predicting the demand for life insurance is to find any changes in ownership of life insurance. Therefore, it is possible to make the argument that ANN estimation offers better predicting performance for the demand for life insurance. The results imply that the variable list derived from

**Table 6.20** RMSE comparison result by logistic model and ANN (Clusters A, B, and C)

| | *Estimation* | *Drop* | *No change* | *Purchase* |
|---|---|---|---|---|
| Cluster A | Logit | .0972 | .1247 | .0863 |
| ($n$=787) | ANN | .0490 | .0876 | .0522 |
| Cluster B | Logit | .0969 | .1418 | .1169 |
| ($n$=1186) | ANN | .0512 | .0795 | .0452 |
| Cluster C | Logit | .1593 | .2104 | .1490 |
| ($n$=317) | ANN | .0450 | .0770 | .0576 |

the ANN estimation is more powerful in predicting the probability of demand for life insurance in the future. Considering that the list found by the ANN estimation indicates the basic combination of impactful influential variables (i.e., shared covariance) regardless of marginal effect, the combination makes an improvement of prediction on the demand for life insurance.

## 6.11 Summary

This chapter provided the results of the analysis. The chapter described the sample and sampling procedure, the data split, the procedure of estimation/prediction, and findings. To summarize, looking over all the characteristics of the sample (i.e., individual characteristics, family characteristics, microenvironmental characteristics, and macroenvironmental characteristics), the sample generally represented the US population. Using a clustering analysis method, the sample was divided into five groups that were reduced to three: (a) low wealth single females, (b) average household, and (c) wealthy large families. Two wealthy groups were too small to investigate statistically. Excluding those two groups, estimations and predictions were conducted. In order to find appropriate models and to check prediction levels, the sample data were divided into two datasets. The first dataset was the training dataset with 2278 respondents. The second dataset was the testing dataset with 2290 respondents. Using the first dataset, it was possible to obtain logistic estimations with odds ratios and to find ANN estimations with prominent weight values. By utilizing the second dataset and estimations, it was possible to predict the probability of the demand for life insurance. As the estimation/prediction showed, each cluster had a different list of influential variables on the demand for life insurance. In addition, each estimation procedure (i.e., logistic and ANN) showed a different list of influential variables that were associated with the demand for life insurance. The different variable lists were caused by the different treatment of covariance (unique covariance and shared covariance) in the approaches. Finally, the study found that the ANN prediction procedure, utilizing prominent variables from the ANN estimation, was better in predicting the probability of demand for life insurance. The next chapter discusses implication of these results.

## References


Burnett, J. J., & Palmer, B. A. (1984). Examining life insurance ownership through demographic and psychographic characteristics. *Journal of Risk and Insurance, 51*, 453–467. https://doi.org/10.2307/252479.

Eisenhauer, J. G., & Halek, M. (1999). Prudence, risk aversion, and the demand for life insurance. *Applied Economic Letters, 6*, 239–242. https://doi.org/10.1080/135048599353429.

Fonseca, R., Mullen, K. J., Zamarro, G., & Zissimopoulos, J. (2012). What explains the gender gap in financial literacy? The role of household decision making. *Journal of Consumer Affairs, 46*, 90–106. https://doi.org/10.1111/j.1745-6606.2011.01221.x.

Hammond, J. D., Houston, D. B., & Melander, E. R. (1967). Determinants of household life insurance premium expenditure: An empirical investigation. *Journal of Risk and Insurance, 34*, 397–408. https://doi.org/10.2307/250854.

Hau, A. (2000). Liquidity, estate liquidation, charitable motives, and life insurance demand by retired singles. *The Journal of Risk and Insurance, 67*(1), 123–141. https://doi.org/10.2307/253680.

Heo, W., Grable, J. E., & Chatterjee, S. (2013). Life insurance consumption as a function of wealth change. *Financial Services Review, 22*(4), 389–404.

Lewis, F. D. (1989). Dependents and the demand for life insurance. *American Economic Review, 79*(3), 452–467.

Lyons, A., Neelakantan, U., & Scherpf, E. (2008). Gender and marital differences in wealth and investment decisions. *Journal of Personal Finance, 6*(4), 57–75.

Mantis, G., & Farmer, R. N. (1968). Demand for life insurance. *Journal of Risk and Insurance, 35*, 247–256. https://doi.org/10.2307/250834.

Mirkin, B. (2011). *Core concepts in data analysis: Summarization, correlation and visualization*. New York, NY: Springer.

Saez, E., & Zucman, G. (2014). *Wealth inequality in the United States since 1913: Evidence from capitalized income tax data* (NBEER Working Paper 20625). Retrieved from National Bureau of Economic Research website: http://www.nber.org/papers/w20625.

CHAPTER 7

# Implications and Conclusion: Implications and Conclusion from the Empirical Example of Predicting the Demand for Life Insurance by Using the Dynamic Systemic Framework

**Abstract** In this chapter, there will be theoretical implication and research literature implication. In addition, there will be implications for practitioners and policy makers. Specifically, the implications have empirical observation, which is supported by the next chapter's empirical example.

**Keywords** Demand for life insurance · Dynamic nonlinear systemic approach · Artificial neural network · Implication

This study employed the relatively new theoretical/methodological framework called a dynamic nonlinear systemic framework. The study employed one of the new methodologies in nonlinear estimations, artificial neural network (ANN). By utilizing ANN, the study began with the intent to compare literature related to life insurance demand and linear and nonlinear estimation. The study adds to the literature by advancing theoretical issues, research possibilities, methodological approaches, and practitioner insights.

## 7.1 Theoretical Implications

This study reached the conclusion that the following three theories share a similar approach when explaining consumer behavior: ecological framework, transformative consumer research, and nonlinear science. Based on

© The Author(s) 2020
W. Heo, *The Demand for Life Insurance*,
https://doi.org/10.1007/978-3-030-36903-3_7

these three theories, the study developed a new framework to understand consumer behavior: the dynamic nonlinear systemic framework. The framework was used to estimate the demand for life insurance. Results of the study support the combination of the three theories.

First, the study adopted the systemic approach from the ecological framework. According to the ecological framework, there are many different systems in the real world. These different kinds of systems influence each other intra- or inter-actively. For instance, Deacon and Firebaugh (1988) introduced the concept that there are three systems in actuality: (a) personal system, (b) family system, and (c) ecological system. Influential factors in each system interact inside each system, as well as intra-act across the systems. Following the taxonomy presented by Deacon and Firebaugh, the study categorized possible demand function variables from the literature into four systems: personal system, family system, and two ecological systems (i.e., microenvironmental system and macroenvironmental system). Based on this taxonomy, the study hypothesized that influential variables would interact and intra-act among/across all systems (see Fig. 2.1 in Chapter 2).

The analytical findings of the study showed that the ecological systems are active in practice. As shown in Table 7.1, the prominent influential variables related to the demand for life insurance come from all four systems. White cells in Table 7.1 denote the top ten ranked influential variables. These come from all the systems. Gray cells represent influential variables that were included in the top ranked variables. However, the variables with gray cells still have a positive influential weight value on the demand for life insurance. Black cells are the negative weight value variables. This means that all four systems contain important and influential variables. In addition, prominent influential variables found using ANN estimations had high weight values on the demand for life insurance; it is important to note that they were not listed as significant variables in traditional logistic estimations (see Table 6.10 in Chapter 6). This implies that there are basic variables shared by all households and that influential variables interact within the same system and/or across all systems. In summary, the adoption of the ecological systemic approach was supported by the results of this study.

Second, the study employed the concept of transformative consumer research. According to transformative consumer research, consumer behavior, including the demand for life insurance, can be changed by diverse factors on a continuous basis (Mick, Pettigrew, Pechmann, &

**Table 7.1** Influential variables from the ANN estimation (Clusters A, B, and C)

| *System* | *Measurement* | *Cluster A* | | *Cluster B* | | *Cluster C* | |
|---|---|---|---|---|---|---|---|
| | | *Dr* | *Pur* | *Dr* | *Pur* | *Dr* | *Pur* |
| Individual (human capital) | Education | | | | | | |
| | Existence of training | | | | | | |
| Individual (physical status) | Health interest | | | | | | |
| | Healthy activity | | | | | | |
| | Average drinking | | | | | | |
| Individual (psychological) | Death experience | | | | | | |
| | Sadness | | | | | | |
| | Depression | | | | | | |
| | Risk aversion | | | | | | |
| | Self-esteem | | | | | | |
| Family (structure) | Family size | | | | | | |
| | Marital status | | | | | | |
| | Marital history | | | | | | |
| | Number of children | | | | | | |
| Family (resource) | Family income | | | | | | |
| | Governmental income | | | | | | |
| | Monetary assets | | | | | | |
| | Cash in bonds | | | | | | |
| | Debt status | | | | | | |
| | Credit card debt | | | | | | |
| | Health insurance | | | | | | |
| Family (demographic) | Race | | | | | | |

(continued)

**Table 7.1** (continued)

| | |
|---|---|
| | Gender |
| | Urbanization |
| | Region |
| Microenvironmental | Job history |
| (physical habitat) | Tenure weeks |
| | Job class |
| | Spouse working weeks |
| | Mobility |
| | House ownership |
| Microenvironmental | Religious activity |
| (social aspect) | Community involvement |
| Macroenvironmental | Religious community |
| (sociocultural) | Family conservativeness |
| Macroenvironmental | Welfare rate |
| (political) | Political trend |
| Macroenvironmental | Unemployment weeks |
| (economic) | Economic difficulty |

*Note* White cells denote top ten ranked influential variables; gray cells represent positive impact influential factors out of top ten ranked variable; and black cells are negative impact variables

Ozanne, 2012). In addition, influences on consumers through social structures can be changed by a wide variety of factors as well. The findings of the study support the concept of transformative consumer research. As explained in previous chapters, before the estimation/prediction procedure, the study employed clustering analysis as a way to separate the sample. As shown in Tables 6.4 and 6.5 in Chapter 6, three major clusters emerged. Each had different socio-demographic features. Based on these different socio-demographic features, sub-samples showed different variable impacts on the demand for life insurance (see Table 28). The results support the concept that consumer behavior can be influenced by diverse factors under different social structures.

Third, the study used nonlinear science as a methodological tool. Nonlinear science assumes that reality is too complex to estimate phenomena (e.g., consumer behavior including the demand for life insurance) with linear estimations (Hand, Mannila, & Smyth, 2001; Kudyba, 2014; Linoff & Berry, 2011; Ye, 2014). Similar to adopting theories about complexity (e.g., ecological theory and transformative consumer research), linear estimation can be problematic when investigating the complex world. Specifically, the demand for life insurance is a form of nonlinear behavior, and the best way of understanding this type of consumer behavior is to look at the behavior as probabilistic fluctuations. Therefore, the study utilized a nonlinear estimation, ANN. The results showed that nonlinear estimation is more efficient in terms of probability prediction in the domain of changes in life insurance.

## 7.2 Research Literature Implications

This study helps expand the understanding of what variables influence life insurance demand. As explained in Chapters 3 and 4, previous literature has focused on the marginal effect of variables on the demand for life insurance. Previous findings show positive and negative changes on the demand for life insurance; however, some research has resulted in controversial findings. This study, employing nonlinear estimation (i.e., ANN), changes the viewpoint from marginal effects to impacting weight values on the demand for life insurance. As a result, the combination of changing probabilities and impacting weights enlarges the variable list of the factors associated with the demand for life insurance.

Findings from the previous literature suggest that a limited number of influential variables exist. These include: education, family size or family structure, marital status, religion, spouse working status, income, net worth, employment, and inflation or interest rates. However, by utilizing a traditional logistic model with sub-sampling (i.e., combination of clustering analysis and logistic estimation), it was possible to find a more significant influential list of variables for each particular sub-sample. Specifically, three clusters emerged from this study: low wealth single female, average consumers, and wealthy consumers with large families. Twenty-three items were found to be significantly associated with dropping and purchasing life insurance using logistic estimation. Findings suggest that the marginal effect of some influential variables can vary by socioeconomic sub-samples.

In addition, utilizing nonlinear estimation with sub-sampling (i.e., combination of clustering analysis and ANN) identified more influential items related to dropping and purchasing life insurance. The difference between the lists produced by logistic estimation and ANN estimation is that (a) variables found using logistic estimation had only a marginal effect on the dropping and purchasing life insurance, whereas (b) variables found using ANN showed the basic combination of influential variables associated with dropping and purchasing life insurance. Because of the difference, the prediction levels using ANN estimation showed better performance than the prediction level using logistic estimation.

## 7.3 Methodological Implications

Logistic estimation is a more efficient method if a researcher's goal is to find the marginal effect of variables because the logistic function calculates partial coefficients using a unique covariance between a specific independent variable and targeted dependent variable. However, if more variables are included in a linear estimation model, the size of unique covariance gets smaller. This is the reason why the variables found in previous studies often are conflicting (see Table 1.1 in Chapter 1). Also, this is the reason why the variables reported in previous studies are sometimes different from the variables described using this study's logistic estimations (see Table 7.1). ANN estimations are more focused on high impacting variables helping shape the demand for life insurance. Specifically, the ANN estimation used here and used the shared covariance among all input variables. Using this method, it was possible to find more important variables which were hidden in linear estimations (see Table 6.19 in Chapter 6). In this sense, prominent influential variables become the foundation for understanding the demand for life insurance. Few of the variables found using the ANN estimation matched the variables identified using logistic procedures. This means that those unmatched but important variables existed as shared covariance. They had an influential weight on the demand for life insurance but were not calculated using logistic estimation. As a result, it was concluded that linear estimation, like logistic methods, is more efficient in finding marginal effects but less efficient in finding basic impacting variables. Nonlinear estimation (e.g., ANN) is more powerful in predicting the probability of change in demand for life insurance than linear estimation. To sum up, the study found that nonlinear estimation shows better performance in finding core demand variables and predicting the future demand for life insurance. This finding contributes to the scholarly literature by helping explain and predict consumer behavior as it relates to life insurance decisions.

## 7.4 Implications for Practitioners and Policy Makers

Financial planners play an important role in providing advice about the purchase of appropriate life insurance policies based on their clients' socioeconomic situation. Financial planners need tools to predict which people will likely drop or purchase life insurance in the future. In addition, they need to know what kinds of factors are associated with purchasing behavior. To this point, financial planners may use the findings from this study to better understand more about why people drop or purchase life insurance. The high impact weight variables from the study can be used to gauge future behavior. This study used a clustering analysis before executing the main estimations and predictions. By using clusters, the study found that different socio-demographic populations have varying reasons for engaging in life insurance behaviors.

Each consumer group has a different unique foundation of variables that influence decision to drop or purchase life insurance. As shown in Figs. 7.1 and 7.2, each consumer group has a unique influential variable list. When financial planners consult their clients, they should attempt to classify their clients into an appropriate socioeconomic profile (e.g., Clusters A, B, and C). They should also consider the leading variables that influence that particular cluster as profile.

Four top ranked variables were found to influence respondents' decision to drop life insurance among those in Cluster A: ethnicity (Hispanic), self-employment job class, marital history, and sadness. Six top ranked variables were found to influence respondents' life insurance purchase decision for those in Cluster A: self-esteem, mobility, governmental income, number of children, living in urban area but not in central city, and unemployment weeks. In terms of insurance planning, a financial planner needs to consider the probability of behavioral changes among this specific group of clients (i.e., low wealth single females) with these four and six top ranked variables. For instance, Hispanic

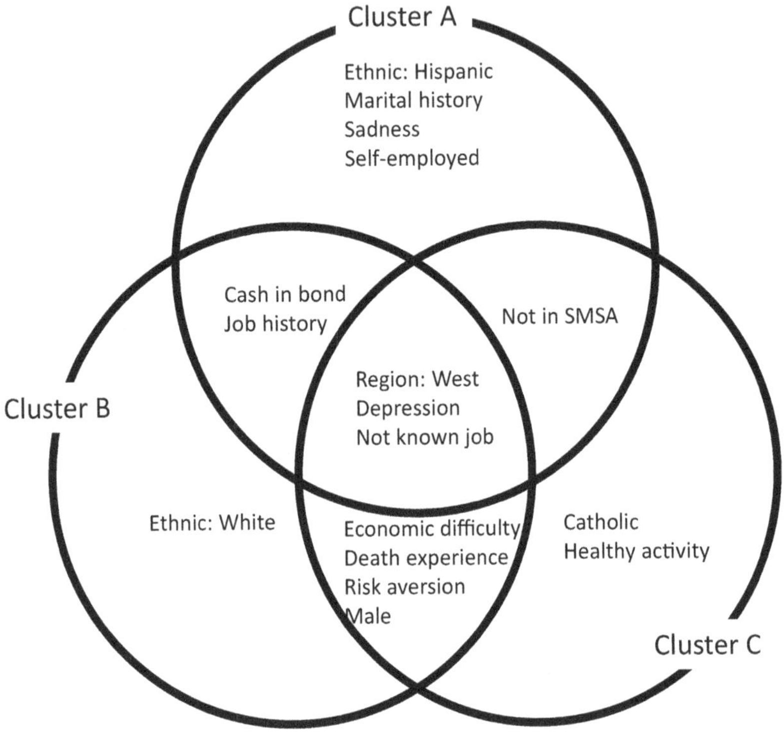


**Fig. 7.1** Top weighted value variables associated with dropping life insurance among Clusters A, B, and C

clients, who are also low wealth single females, are more likely to drop their life insurance than other clients. If a client is self-employed, then the client might show a higher possibility to drop life insurance than other job class workers. More frequencies in marital history or greater self-reported sadness are likely to drive these clients to drop life insurance in future. Conversely, a client having high self-esteem or more children would likely purchase life insurance in the future. Those who move more frequently and those who have governmental income are likely to have a higher intention to purchase life insurance. Also, external factors like living in an urban area and a more unstable job market (i.e., unemployment weeks of living region) are possible factors associated with purchasing life insurance.

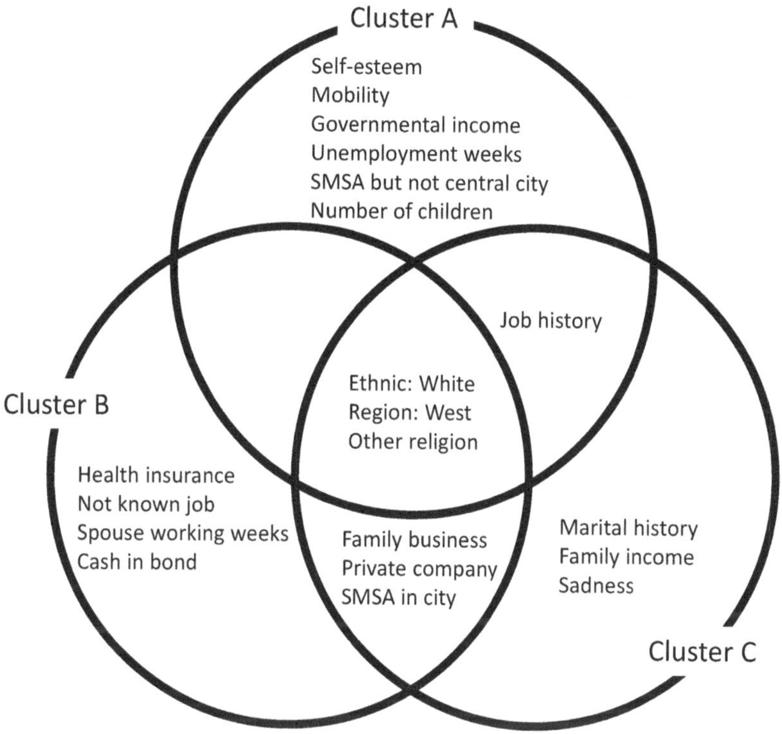


**Fig. 7.2** Top weighted value variables associated with purchasing life insurance among Clusters A, B, and C

Several factors were found to have relevance only among those in Cluster B. Being White influences the decision to drop life insurance and four variables (i.e., health insurance, not known job class, spouse working weeks, and cash in bond) affect the purchasing decision. Similar to the case of Cluster A, financial planners need to consider these foundation variables when predicting who is likely to drop or purchase life insurance among average consumers (i.e., Cluster B). For instance, White consumers are more likely to drop life insurance than others. In addition, consumers who have health insurance are more likely to purchase life insurance in future. Those who have more cash in bonds or those who have a spouse working more weeks show a higher likelihood of purchasing life insurance in future. Financial planners should consider these findings when they consult their clients on the topic of insurance planning. Specifically, the combination of weight values and ANN formula (see function [5.3] in Chapter 5) may be utilized to estimate drop and purchase probability. If a client from average consumers group (i.e., Cluster B) is (a) being White, (b) having a health insurance, (c) having more cash in bonds, and (d) having more spouse working weeks, then the formula may be written like below:

$$\begin{aligned}\Pr(\text{Drop}) = {} & 5.59 \times 1(\text{White}) \\ & + (-9.36) \times 1(\text{health insurance}) \\ & + 6.40 \times (\text{Dollar in bonds}) \\ & + (-7.23) \times (\text{Number of spouse working weeks}) \\ & + \sum (\text{Other factors} \times \text{weight values})\end{aligned} \tag{7.1}$$

$$\begin{aligned}\Pr(\text{Pur}) = {} & 8.53 \times 1(\text{White}) \\ & + 4.79 \times 1(\text{health insurance}) \\ & + 1.92 \times (\text{Dollar in bonds}) \\ & + 3.57 \times (\text{Number of spouse working weeks}) \\ & + \sum (\text{Other factors} \times \text{weight values})\end{aligned} \tag{7.2}$$

For instance, an observation with (a) being White, (b) having a health insurance, (c) having high cash in bonds (e.g., \$350,000), and (d) having high spouse working weeks (e.g., 52 weeks) showed 5.97% dropping probability and 12.79% purchasing probability by the calculations. The actual observed average probability in Cluster B was 10.96% for drop life insurance and 10.46% for purchase life insurance (see Table 6.16 in Chapter 6). Therefore, financial planners can expect lower dropping probability and higher purchasing probability when consulting a client with the specific conditions.

Some factors were shown to be associated only among those in Cluster C. Those who report their religion as Catholic and those who report being healthy are more likely to drop life insurance in the future. Considering that Cluster C consisted of wealthy consumers with larger families, mainstream religious affiliations and healthy activities may prompt them to regard life insurance as a less valuable protection tool for future risk. In other words, those with higher wealth might regard cash value life insurance as a substitute to their wealth. On the other hand, those who have more frequent marital history or those who have more family income are more likely to purchase life insurance. Financial planners need to understand what variables drive wealthy consumers to drop life insurance or purchase life insurance.

In addition to the unique foundation variable lists for each cluster, financial planners should consider the common variables that influence dropping life insurance across clusters. For instance, cash in bonds and job history influenced the dropping behavior across Clusters A and B. Average or low wealth consumers' concern about the dollar amount they have in bonds or the stability of their jobs may prompt dropping coverage. Average or low wealth consumers with more cash in bonds and with more frequent changes in their jobs show a greater likelihood of dropping life insurance. In addition, living in rural area (i.e., not in SMSA) influenced the decision to drop coverage across Clusters A and C. These types of extreme consumers-those with low wealth or high wealth-living in rural areas have more likelihood to be independent. Furthermore, four variables (i.e., death experience, economic difficulty, male, and risk aversion) were found to affect coverage behavior across Clusters B and C. Consumers with relatively reliable wealth seem to be more influenced by psychological factors, like a death experience (i.e., regret) and risk aversion. Also, economic difficulty drives them to drop life insurance.

Financial planners should consider the common variables that influence purchasing life insurance across clusters as well. Between Clusters A and C, job history was found to influence purchasing behavior. Frequent job changes in the past are linked with purchasing life insurance. This implies that more changes in jobs among those in Clusters A and C may cause them to worry about future income. Between Clusters B and C, three variables (i.e., family business worker, private company worker, and living in urban area) were found to influence the demand for life insurance. Considering that these two groups have relatively stable wealth, their current job class and living environment appear to be the main reasons to purchase life insurance in future. An interesting point is that there is no common variable between Clusters A and B in terms of purchasing life insurance. This implies that these two groups have totally different behavior.

Across Clusters A, B, and C, there are some common variables that influence dropping or purchasing life insurance. Financial planners should understand the influence of these common foundation variables when consulting their clients. Three foundation variables influence the decision to drop life insurance across Clusters A, B, and C: not known job class, west region, and depression. In particular, depression is an important factor. Clients that exhibit depression symptoms should be referred to a specialist and counseled an importance of life insurance as a risk management tool. Financial planners should understand the point and consult their clients. Another three foundation variables also affect the decision to purchase life insurance across Clusters A, B, and C: other religious community, White, and west region. White consumers are more likely to purchase life insurance. Having another religion influence also increases the likelihood of purchasing life insurance in future. The interesting point is that living in the west region is a common variable across all clusters and all behaviors. This implies that consumers living in the west region show more dynamic life insurance behavior.

Second, in terms of the perspective of policy makers, it is important to discuss the role of life insurance within a consumer's financial well-being profile. Generally, life insurance is used as a precaution for an unexpected event like the premature death of a family's breadwinner (Rejda, 2008; Thoyts, 2010). Losing a household's breadwinner increases the financial vulnerability of a family. Although the person who dies may not be the household's breadwinner, the loss of a related family member may increase economic burdens on the other members in the household. Viewing households as individuals, it is important to predict which people are cautious and which people are not. Therefore, policy makers have a need to understand the reason why people discontinue or purchase life insurance. For instance, policy makers should notice and consider the variables related to dropping coverage:

(a) four variables affecting only Cluster A (i.e., Hispanic, marital history, self-employment, and sadness);
(b) one variable affecting only Cluster B (i.e., White);
(c) two variables affecting only Cluster C (i.e., Catholic and healthy activity);
(d) two variables affecting both Clusters A and B (i.e., cash in bond and job history);
(e) one variable affecting both Clusters A and C (i.e., not in SMSA);
(f) four variables affecting both Clusters B and C (i.e., death experience, economic difficulty, male, and risk aversion);
(g) three variables affecting all consumers (i.e., not known job class, west region, and depression).

Results from this study are strongly associated with political issues, such as Social Security funding (Black & Skipper, 2000). As a result, policy makers can use the results to monitor the life insurance market and help the market work efficiently and effectively in order to secure consumer well-being. The findings from this study support better prediction performance on the demand for life insurance so policy makers can better know which variables are the foundation for dropping and purchasing life insurance.

## 7.5 Conclusion, Limitation, and Further Direction

Life insurance is an important financial product for households as a protection against the possible premature death of a household member. Therefore, it is important to understand the demand for life insurance, as well as predict consumer behavior associated with the ownership of life insurance. In previous approaches to understand the demand for life insurance, perspectives from actuarial science and life-span economics have generally employed. However, previous research literature has shown inconsistent findings. The inconsistent results were caused by two factors: (a) Research models did not always match the theories and (b) researchers sometimes exhibited indifference toward interdependent correlations among influential variables. In order to perform a better prediction of the demand for life insurance, this study explored three theories: ecological systemic theory, transformative consumer research, and dynamic nonlinear science in economic areas. Ecological systemic theory shows that diverse influential variables possibly interact and intra-act among and across systems. Based on ecological systemic theory, it was determined that diverse possible influential variables should be included in estimation and prediction analyses. Nonlinear science supports the statistical method used in this study-ANN.

In the procedure of analysis, the study split the data into two sets. The first dataset was a training set to estimate models. The second dataset was a testing set to check the performance of predictions. In addition, the study employed clustering analysis to create a sub-sampling of all respondents since the assumption of the study was that people do not have the same reasons to own life insurance. By executing the clustering analysis, the study yielded three significant groups: low wealth single females, average consumers, and wealthy people with large families. Utilizing the three sub-samples with the two datasets, the study estimated and predicted the demand for life insurance with two different estimations. The first one was a linear estimation using multinomial logistic modeling. The second one was nonlinear estimation using ANN modeling.

The results are both interesting and noteworthy. Each cluster had its own foundation variables for prediction life insurance coverage. Also, there were common foundation variables across two or three clusters for the prediction of dropping or purchasing life insurance. Finding showed that some specific variables influence a particular consumer group and some common variables affect larger common consumer groups. In addition, prediction using ANN showed considerably smaller RMSE estimates. This means that prediction using ANN is more efficient compared to linear estimation. Understanding that linear estimation focuses on marginal effects with partial covariance, the linear estimation was found to be more efficient in finding a specific variable's marginal impact on the demand for life insurance. However, the nonlinear estimation was more efficient as a way to understand which variables had a shared covariance with other variables associated with the demand for life insurance. Because of the different efficiencies related to finding marginal effects and impact weights on the demand for life insurance, nonlinear estimation with ANN was found to provide better performance when predicting the probability of dropping and purchasing life insurance.

The findings from the study have diverse implications. First, the results showed the value of combining pre-existing theories (e.g., ecological systemic theory, transformative consumer research, and nonlinear science) and expanding them into a new conceptual framework, dynamic nonlinear systemic model. Second, the study identified the important variables shaping the demand for life insurance. In general, shared covariance is automatically dropped by linear functions. However, ANN estimation identified important variables and predicted the change in demand for life insurance better than linear estimation. Third, the study illustrates the possibility of using nonlinear estimation in financial planning. Finally, the study provided a list of important variables to be used by practitioners and policy makers so that they may understand the demand for life insurance better than before.

Although the findings from this study are meaningful, there are a few limitations associated with this study. First, in this study, only cash value life insurance was observed. Term life insurance is mainly designed to protect current wealth against future possible risk. Group life insurance is mainly consumed by those who are employed. Cash value life insurance, on the other hand, is designed to combine protection and investment. Therefore, the demand for this type of life insurance can be different, which is the reason this study narrowed down the topic to cash value life insurance. Second, the original clusters were included groups. However, the fourth and fifth clusters represented the top 1% wealthy consumer group. The sample sizes were too small ($n=93$ and $n=19$, respectively). Considering that logistic and ANN estimation procedure split the observations into two datasets (i.e., training dataset and testing dataset), the observation numbers were too small to execute logistic and ANN estimation. Future studies should evaluate ANN estimation with these clusters. Third, other ethnic groups (i.e., Asian, native Hawaiian or Pacific Islander, American Indian or Alaska native, and other race) were not included in logistic and ANN estimation because of their small number in observations ($n=10$, $n=4$, $n=31$, and $n=22$, respectively). With an appropriate dataset, and a future study, there might be better interpretation about the dismissed two clusters and diverse ethnic groups.

Based on this study, the next research can take a step to further understand the demand for life insurance. For instance, this study used a two-period dataset from 2008 to 2012; however, with the most updated survey data, the next study can confirm the ANN estimation and resulting predictions. In addition, based on the findings from the study, it may be possible to assume more precise associations among independent variables shaping the demand for life insurance. For instance, it may be possible to estimate structural equation models by using variables found using ANN estimation in this study. The variable lists found using ANN denote the shared covariance factors, which could be possibly assumed to be moderating or mediating behind the direct association between some significant variables found using logistic and the demand for life insurance. Furthermore, the improvement in predicting the demand for life insurance in this study opens a gate to employ nonlinear estimation in the field of family and consumer science and financial planning. In other words, nonlinear estimation, like ANN estimation and prediction, can likely be used in other behavioral research in the field of family and consumer science. This possibility should be explored in more detail.

## References


Black, K., & Skipper, H. D. (2000). *Life & health insurance* (13th ed.). Upper Saddle River, NJ: Prentice Hall.

Deacon, R. E., & Firebaugh, F. M. (1988). *Family resource management: Principles and applications* (2nd ed.). Boston, MA: Allyn & Bacon.

Hand, D., Mannila, H., & Smyth, P. (2001). *Principles of data mining*. Cambridge, MA: MIT Press.

Kudyba, S. (2014). *Big data, mining, and analytics* (S. Kudyba, Ed.). Boca Raton, FL: CRC Press, Taylor & Francis.

Linoff, G. S., & Berry, M. J. A. (2011). *Data mining techniques: For marketing, sales, and customer relationship management* (3rd ed.). Indianapolis, IN: Wiley.

Mick, D. G., Pettigrew, S., Pechmann, C., & Ozanne, J. L. (Eds.). (2012). *Transformative consumer research for personal and collective well-being*. New York, NY: Taylor & Francis.

Rejda, G. E. (2008). *Principles of risk management and insurance* (10th ed.). Boston, MA: Pearson Addison-Wesley.

Thoyts, R. (2010). *Insurance theory and practice*. New York: Routledge, NY.

Ye, N. (2014). *Data mining: Theories, algorithms, and examples*. Boca Raton, FL: CRC Press and Taylor & Francis Group.

# Index



© The Editor(s) (if applicable) and The Author(s), under exclusive license to Springer Nature Switzerland AG 2020
W. Heo, *The Demand for Life Insurance*,
https://doi.org/10.1007/978-3-030-36903-3

The manufacturer's authorised representative in the EU is Springer Nature Customer Service Centre GmbH, Europaplatz 3, 69115 Heidelberg, Germany. If you have any concerns regarding our products, please contact ProductSafety@springernature.com

Printed and bound by CPI Group (UK) Ltd, Croydon, CR0 4YY
05/10/2026
02227715-0001